Interpreting Native American History and Culture at Museums and Historic Sites

INTERPRETING HISTORY

About the Series

The American Association for State and Local History publishes the *Interpreting History* series in order to provide expert, in-depth guidance in interpretation for history professionals at museums and historic sites. The books are intended to help practioners expand their interpretation to be more inclusive of the range of American history.

Books in this series help readers:

- quickly learn about the questions surrounding a specific topic,
- introduce them to the challenges of interpreting this part of history, and
- highlight best practice examples of how interpretation has been done by different organizations.

They enable institutions to place their interpretative efforts into a larger context, despite each having a specific and often localized mission. These books serve as quick references to practical considerations, further research, and historical information.

Titles in the Series

Interpreting Native American History and Culture at Museums and Historic Sites by Raney Bench
Interpreting the Prohibition Era by Jason D. Lantzer
Interpreting African American History and Culture at Museums and Historic Sites by Max van Balgooy

Interpreting Native American History and Culture at Museums and Historic Sites

By Raney Bench

ROWMAN & LITTLEFIELD
Lanham • Boulder • New York • London

To my husband, John, for loving and supporting me and giving me the space to write. To our boys, Oakley and Emery, for their laughter and snuggles. And to my parents, for everything.

Published by Rowman & Littlefield
A wholly owned subsidiary of The Rowman & Littlefield Publishing Group, Inc.
4501 Forbes Boulevard, Suite 200, Lanham, Maryland 20706
www.rowman.com

16 Carlisle Street, London W1D 3BT, United Kingdom

British Library Cataloguing in Publication Information Available

Library of Congress Cataloging-in-Publication Data
Bench, Raney.
Interpreting Native American history and culture at museums and historic sites / Raney Bench.
pages cm
Summary: "Interpreting Native American History and Culture at Museums and Historic Sites features ideas and suggested best practices for the staff and board of museums that care for collections of Native material culture, and who work with Native American culture, history, and communities}—Provided by publisher.
Includes bibliographical references and index.
ISBN 978-0-7591-2337-3 (cloth : alkaline paper) — ISBN 978-0-7591-2338-0 (paperback : alkaline paper) — ISBN 978-0-7591-2339-7 (electronic) 1. Indians of North America—Museums. 2. Indians of North America—Historiography. 3. Indians of North America—Government relations. 4. Indians of North America—Material culture. 5. Museums and Indians—United States. 6. Museums and community—United States. I. Title.
E76.85.B46 2014
970.004'97—dc23 2014023908

∞™ The paper used in this publication meets the minimum requirements of American National Standard for Information Sciences—Permanence of Paper for Printed Library Materials, ANSI/NISO Z39.48-1992.

Printed in the United States of America

Contents

Preface vii

Acknowledgments xvii

CHAPTER 1 **Knowing the History: A Brief History of Federal Indian Policy** 1

CHAPTER 2 **Getting Started** 15

CHAPTER 3 **Consultation with Tribes and Advice from the Field: Citizen Potawatomi National Cultural Heritage Center** 25
Kelli Mosteller and R. Blake Norton

CHAPTER 4 **Building Partnerships and Authority Sharing** 35

Case Study: *Native Voices*: A Permanent Gallery at the Natural History Museum of Utah 43
Becky Menlove

CHAPTER 5 **Taking Responsibility for Museum History and Legacy: Promoting Change in Collections Management** 57

Case Study: The Abbe Museum: Seeking a Collaborative Future through Decolonization 65
Darren Ranco and Julia Clark

CHAPTER 6 **Establishing Tribal Partners in Education and Public Programs** 77

Case Study: Portland Art Museum: *Object Stories*: Connecting Collections with Communities 86

Deana Dartt and Michael Murawski

CHAPTER 7 **Pulling It All Together: Native Advisory Councils and Governance** 97

Case Study: Collaborating with Cultures: The Eiteljorg Museum of American Indians and Western Art 104

James H. Nottage

CHAPTER 8 **Review and Final Thoughts** 115

Appendix 1
Timeline of Selected Federal Indian Policies, Laws, and Court Cases 119

Appendix 2
Activity to Understand Stereotype and Bias 125

Index 127

About the Author 129

Preface

Interpreting Native American History and Culture at Museums and Historic Sites features ideas and suggested best practices for the staff and board of museums that care for collections of Native material culture and who work with Native American culture, history, and communities. The goal is to give museum staff and board members benchmarks to help shape conversations and policies designed to improve relations with Native communities represented in the museum. In the pages that follow, museums that are purposefully working to incorporate Native people and perspectives into all aspects of their work share experiences, hoping to inspire other museum staff to reach out to tribes to develop or improve their own interpretative processes.

This book does not address the legal requirements for working with tribes related to the Native American Graves Protection and Repatriation Act (NAGPRA). There have been many books, articles, and studies written about NAGPRA, from both museum and tribal perspectives. The steps outlined by NAGPRA and the communication it has created between tribes and museums are important, and in many cases, have been transformative for both museums and tribes. The law mandates interaction between museums that hold Native collections and the tribes those objects came from, but this does not represent best practices for interpreting Native history and culture.

This book strives to go beyond the law, to generate discussions about how to work collaboratively, share authority, and incorporate multiple ways of knowing about the past into all interpretation about Native people, objects, history, and culture. Each Native Nation is unique, and each relationship is different, making it difficult to provide concrete answers or a systematic approach. The chapters that follow provide a framework for thinking about and building relations with Native communities.

Can a museum accurately interpret another culture? We can share facts, opinions, events, and perspectives, but only someone from within a culture can truly know it, and even then, maybe only aspects of it. The responsibility to share one's culture rests with the individuals who are members of that culture, and when appropriate, in partnership with museums, cultural centers, and other outsiders. For generations, Native people have not been allowed the authority to share their culture by their choice. Instead, Native people have often been on the outside, watching while others interpreted objects, ceremonies, and relationships—at times incorrectly. The tide has turned, and collaboration with Native people is now common, primarily in exhibit development, but in other aspects of museum work as well. That said, there is a lot of room for improvement, and the process of implementing best practices is ongoing.

Native people are not minorities in a community whose stories come and go with population shifts. They are indigenous to this land and continue to play an important and transformational role in American society. Native people are members of sovereign nations, whose borders cross with those of the United States, Mexico, and Canada in complex and often misunderstood ways. The more their voices, perspectives, and experiences are shared, the more we learn about our shared history and ourselves. And the more Native people have the opportunity to share their knowledge and values, the more their communities and traditions live and thrive. "Heritage work, to the extent that it selectively preserves and updates cultural traditions and relations to place, can be part of a social process that strengthens indigenous claims to deep roots—to a status beyond that of another minority or local interest group."[1] First, an explanation of what is meant by the terms *interpretation* and *Native American*.

A Discussion about Language

What Do We Mean by *Interpretation*?

One definition of interpretation commonly used in Canada is "Interpretation is a communication process, designed to reveal meanings and relationships of our cultural and natural heritage, through involvement with objects, artifacts, landscapes and sites."[2] The challenge with this definition is that it does not include people—as interpreters or as the beneficiaries of interpretation. "It should be stressed that interpretive communications is not simply presenting information, but a specific communication strategy that is used to translate that information for people, from the technical language of the expert, to the everyday language of the visitor."[3]

The East Side Tenement Museum handbook for interpretation offers this definition "Interpretation . . . is foremost an educational activity that works to promote civic engagement and significant understanding about culture, both past and present. Through various experiences—including talks, guided tours, and exhibits—interpretation effectively develops an understanding and appreciation of historic sites."[4]

In 1957 Freeman Tilden wrote *Interpreting Our Heritage*, which remains an important work defining the principles and practices of interpretation. In it, Tilden outlines several principles of interpretation, which are still widely cited. Tilden's principles state that for interpretation to be meaningful to visitors, the display or description needs to relate to a personal experience or the personality of the visitor. In addition, Tilden explains that "Information, as such, is not interpretation. Interpretation is revelation based upon information. But they are entirely different things. However, all interpretation includes information. Interpretation should aim to present a whole rather than a part."[5] This last point is particularly salient when considering interpretation about Native people.

Indian or Native American?

There are many terms used to describe the first people to live in North America, and it can be confusing to know which terms are acceptable to use or not. The term *Indian* is the legal word used in federal Indian law and policy, the constitution, and in some treaties. Many indigenous people in the United States grew up using the term *Indian*, and for some tribes, it is incorporated into their legal name or the name of the tribal community. With the rise of the American Indian Movement (AIM) during the civil rights era, the federal government came up with the term *Native American*, in an attempt to "to recognize the primacy of indigenous peoples' tenure in the nation."[6] Many people, including indigenous people, started using this term, and though it remains popular, it has never been fully adopted among indigenous people. It has been argued that this term allows non-Native people to ignore painful histories of Indian–white relations. The term *Indian* is loaded with the history of colonization, and some indigenous people feel it is important to remind non-Native people about that history through continued use of the term *Indian*. It can also be argued that anyone born in the United States, or in the Americas, is a native of America, and therefore the term *Native American* can be confusing. In Canada, Native people are referred to as "First Nations," but it is not a term used in the United States.

American Indian became popular among Native people at the same time that Native American began being used, but it has not caught on with non-Native people as much. There is a feeling that American Indian better expresses the status of indigenous people in the United States because it is the only race in which the term *American* comes first. Currently, the term *Native* is popular among both Native and non-Native communities.

As a rule of thumb, it is best to refer to a person or a community by the name of the specific tribe. Many tribes have officially changed their name, returning to a more traditional way of identifying the community. Some tribal names such as Papago, as one example, were how European explorers or colonial forces referred to a tribe. Sometimes those forces learned that name from a neighboring tribe rather than the tribe itself, or the name is a derogatory term used by regional enemies. These names were not the name a tribe called itself. During the Indian self-determination movement of the 1960s, many tribes openly reconnected with their traditions, language, and history for the first time in generations. As a result, some tribes have changed the legal tribal name, or spelling, to reflect traditional terms and indigenous language. The Papago have returned to their traditional name, Tohono O'odham. Before reaching out to a tribe, it is important to do a little research into the name and spelling they prefer to use.

When referring to more than one tribe or a group of Native people from different communities, a more general term is required. There are confederations of tribes in many parts of the country, and these terms are acceptable when talking about Native people from the region. For example, the Wabanaki is a confederacy of five Nations working together in partnership, so when referring to the indigenous people of northern New England and the Canadian Maritimes, this term is appropriate. Confederated tribes often share some cultural and linguistic characteristics, and because of the status of the confederation, work together as a political body. It is acceptable, and often appropriate, to use the term for the confederacy when referring to regional groups.

Finally, if a need to generalize and group all Native people together becomes necessary, as in this book, larger terms are needed, such as Indian, Native American, American Indian, and Native. You will find all of these terms used interchangeably throughout the book. When working with Native people, pay attention to body language and other clues that might indicate if there is a preference for any of these terms. I have worked with Native people who are comfortable with all of the preceding terms, and others who prefer to be identified only by their tribal name. As with all people, each person is different and brings a different perspective and set of experiences with them, so be courteous and sensitive to their preferences.

How the United States Government Defines American Indian Tribes

Within the broader terms of Indian and so forth, there are additional terms that are important to know when working with Native people. At the time of European contact, all Native communities were sovereign, having created their own governments and civic systems, languages, values, and political alliances. Chapter 1 provides a summary of how Native, European, and the United States have interacted in the past and the basis of the current relationship between Indian Nations and the US government.

Today, there are more than 560 federally recognized tribes in the United States. Federal recognition is granted to a tribal government that can prove it has maintained a continuous government since 1900, that it has maintained political influence over its members, and that it has membership criteria, among other things. Most federally recognized tribes have been recognized since European contact, based on alliances, treaty agreements, and assertion of their sovereignty. All tribes have suffered devastating population loss and upheaval as a result of colonialism, but some tribes were also removed from their home territories or were absorbed into other tribal and nontribal communities as a means of survival. For these tribes, who could not maintain sovereign status, there is an application and review process that, if successful, can lead to recognition. Tribes with federal recognition are subject to federal Indian policy and have a direct relationship with the federal government.

There are tribes who do not have federal recognition but are recognized as a sovereign political entity by the state in which they reside. The relationships between tribes and state governments differ, depending on the state, so research into the rights and responsibilities of state-recognized tribes is helpful before embarking on a new relationship.

Finally, there are tribal communities that are not recognized by either federal or state governments. This poses challenges for everyone involved. Unfortunately, there are non-Native people who appropriate Native culture and identity and try to claim the distinct status, rights, and recognition that Native people have retained. At the same time, years of forced assimilation policies have had a deep impact on Native identity. There are Native people who hid their heritage from everyone for safety; there were thousands of children who were forcibly removed from their homes and sent far away to boarding schools; and there are families who were paid to leave the reservation and move to faraway cities in an effort to break traditional systems of education. As a result, who is and who is not Native is not always clear. Federal and state recognition are helpful, but they are a continuation of a system of colonization and dominance that has assumed the authority to define Native sovereignty. On the other hand, federally recognized tribes can see the value in a rigorous process for defining sovereign nations, which in some ways protects the integrity of the government-to-government relationship.

When working with Native communities, be aware of these status issues, and of the potential for Native imposters to approach the museum to present programs, to ask for their works to be included in collections or in the shop, or for other partnerships. If you are uncertain or question the authenticity of someone claiming to be Native, contact the tribe this person claims to be from to verify his or her identity and ability to represent the tribe.

Museums and Native Communities: An Uneasy History

"Native Americas have a tortured relationship with museums. Museums offer significant bodies of scholarship and knowledge that cannot be discounted; nevertheless, museological practices are underpinned by Western epistemologies, systems of classification, and ideological assumptions that, when applied to Native Americans, have functioned in exploitive, objectifying, and demeaning ways."[7]

When interpreting American Indian material culture or history, museums have a long history of excluding Native people from the process. Starting with the earliest collecting practices and public exhibits, American Indian history and culture have been interpreted by outsiders. "The relationship between Native American peoples and museums spans centuries and has varied so extensively that it nearly defies general description. However, because American museums are a part of our social fabric, museum narratives and practices are informed by overall social perceptions of Native peoples. The stereotypes inherent in historic museum representations of "Indianness" have repeatedly overwritten the existence and persistence of actual Native American communities."[8]

Europeans started collecting Native American objects as soon as they began traveling to and from North America. A more detailed summary of collecting practices can be found in chapter 5. Thomas Jefferson's entryway at Monticello may have been the "nation's first museum of the American Indian."[9] Jefferson displayed artifacts collected from Lewis and Clark and also archaeological artifacts found during his research into the origins of American Indians in the Western Hemisphere.

American Indian human remains were collected and housed in museums to be studied for evidence of inferiority based on their biology. These studies became the basis for federal Indian policy, which argued that skull analysis proved that the small cranial capacity of Indians "reflected an unusually uniform mental makeup. The rather small cranial capacity not only betrayed an intellect inferior to other races, but the other cranial indicators necessary for the predilection for the arts or sciences were entirely absent."[10] This prevailing, colonial, perception of Indians as inferior dominated the academic and political conversations about Indians in the United States and excluded the perspective of Indians themselves.

As museums became part of the fabric of American cities, and collectors sought objects and art to decorate their homes and offices, Native craft, lifestyles, and clothing were documented as part of the process. Sometimes Native informants were interviewed about the use of the objects collected, other times they were not, and white collectors made conclusions about the use or creation process based on observation and guesswork.

In the early 1900s, Franz Boas, Frank Speck, and Alfred Kroeber were among many anthropologists working with Indian informants to supplement information about artifacts, lifeways, and document language and stories from what was considered at the time, a "vanishing race."[11] Their work provides important documentation about Indian life in the early twentieth century; however, their conclusions and interpretations are strictly American and colonial. Native informants could provide the raw material, but American anthropologists would interpret its meaning and present their findings to the public through articles, books, lectures, and museum exhibits. Anthropologists who wrote about culture from the perspective of an "insider," including several noted Indian anthropologists and authors, were accused of being biased. Boas and others argued that the study and interpretation of American Indians must be guided by scientific principles to "observe and describe aspects of culture that even those participating in that culture do not know."[12] As a result, Native people were excluded from conversations about their own communities, objects, and values, which were interpreted for the public by outsiders.

If early museums actually wrote labels that interpreted the collections of Native art and craft at all, it often supported stereotypes about Native people—that they were savage, primitive, and vanishing from the landscape. "U.S. museums are critical in upholding certain ideas of the nation, for they are one tool by which a community from divergent backgrounds is able to "imagine" a shared past and future. . . . In most cases, this evolutionary view of cultures excuses conquest and colonialism, presenting such histories as being inevitable (if tragic). Manifest Destiny and perceptions of the frontier contribute to a shared national ignorance of the harm such belief systems have on Indigenous people, as they are translated into policies such as allotment, the reservation system, and boarding schools."[13]

For many Native people, the combined impact of exclusion from the process of documenting and sharing their culture, the repercussions of having significant cultural material removed from their communities, and the pain of seeing beloved ancestors removed from their resting places and housed in museums, fostered negative feelings about museums. "One of the projects, then, is to disrupt institutional structures or representational practices that imply (and therefore reinforce) notions that Native American cultures have been extinguished due to colonizing and acculturating processes."[14]

In the late twentieth century, Indian activists and culture keepers continued the legacy of Indian anthropologists and informants by demanding the right to interpret their own culture, stating that they had not, and had no intention of, vanishing. The rise of American Indian cultural centers is founded on a backlash of this history of exclusion from museum interpretation. "In 1977 the Mohawk of Kahnawake decided to establish a cultural center instead of a museum because they perceived the museum's exclusive focus on the past to be antithetical to their mandate of fostering future cultural development and the revitalization of tradition."[15] Tribal museums and cultural centers have now become common in Indian communities, sometimes for the education of non-Native people about the culture, but oftentimes the focus is for the benefit of the tribal community itself. Courses are held in language, traditional arts and crafts, and feasts, celebrations, and other community events are held in the centers.

Interpretation focuses on telling stories that the community wants to tell about itself, and these exhibits have a distinctly different feel. "Tribal museums are charged with the difficult task of challenging officially sanctioned views of history that most non-Natives unquestioningly believe; simultaneously, they try to create and maintain a place for their own people to learn about their stories of the past."[16]

For nontribal museums, interpreting Native history and culture accurately, and with respect to Native knowledge and perspective, requires effort and outreach. Native people are more involved with museums than ever before and are increasingly part of the museum profession. "Museum theory and practice have made significant strides in revising the relationship between museums and Native Americans, particularly as Native individuals have entered the arena as curators."[17] Authority sharing has led to better balance in interpretation, acknowledging that each party brings a unique perspective in how visitors understand the past or an object. "We are all part of our own culture; my culture places a strong emphasis on scientific research and data. Native American culture places a great emphasis on oral histories and traditional beliefs. Neither is wrong."[18]

Today, there are many nontribal museums that involve Native people on all levels, expanding from the natural opportunities for collaboration in interpretation, to incorporate a more holistic approach to partnerships. With the creation of the National Museum of the American Indian in Washington D.C., a national conversation about the role of Native people in museums and the authority to tell their own stories began. Decolonization has become a buzzword among museums with large Native collections, and much has been written about it over the past couple of years. Winona Wheeler states "Decolonization is about empowerment—a belief that situations can be transformed, a belief and trust in our own peoples' values and abilities and a willingness to make change. It is about transforming negative reactionary energy into the more positive rebuilding energy needed in our communities."[19]

Organizational Structure of the Book

This book will take readers through the beginning stages of working with tribes and forming collaborative relationships, through opportunities to form deeper, more meaningful relationships, until finally, this process is incorporated into all the work that is done. It presents ideas and practices that any museum can implement, whether a small museum with few staff and a limited budget or a large museum with various curatorial departments. It is all about building relationships based on respect, a willingness to take responsibility for the past, and being open to new ways of thinking about and doing museum work.

The first chapter provides a brief overview of some of the more relevant treaties, court cases, and acts of congress that define Indian status in the United States today. It is important to have a basic understanding of the unique status of Native people, and the history of federal Indian relations before embarking on any project with Native communities. Much of this history has been left out of school textbooks, and many people are unaware of how complicated Native American history is.

Chapter 3 is written by staff at the Citizen Potawatomi Nation Cultural Heritage Center, which offers advice for how to start a relationship with a tribe, including who to contact, how to contact people, and some considerations about cultural differences. It also provides examples from the work of the Cultural Heritage Center of successful partnerships and collaborations that were less successful.

The rest of the book alternates between chapters written about specific elements of museum work, describing ideas and methods for working with tribes in relation to collections, exhibits, education, and administration, and case studies relevant to each chapter. Museum professionals and tribal members working in museums in the Northeast, Midwest, Great Plains, and Pacific Northwest wrote the case studies, and they share some of the successes and challenges of their work. Each case study includes background information about the museum, the process by which they began and maintain their relationships with tribal communities, and detailed information about collaborative efforts. The museums represent a wide range of missions, budgets, and collection types. Combined with the Cultural Heritage Center, most regions of the country are represented in an effort to recognize distinctions that may be characteristic for each area. Of course, not all areas or museum types could be addressed, but understanding that each situation and relationship is unique, there are important lessons that can be broadly applied.

Finally, there are two appendixes; one is a timeline of federal Indian policy to use as a reference, and the second is a sample stereotyping activity developed by the staff at the Abbe Museum in partnership with the Penobscot Nation Cultural and Historic Preservation Department. This activity is designed to be used with staff and board members to help recognize stereotypes about Native people and identify ways to correct them.

Notes

1. James Clifford, "Looking Several Ways: Anthropology and Native Heritage in Alaska." *Current Anthroplogy* 45, no. 1 (February 2004): 9.
2. John Vererka and Associates, http://www.heritageinterp.com/whatis.htm.
3. John Vererka et al., http://www.heritageinterp.com/whatis.htm.
4. *Lower East Side Tenement Museum Interpretive Methodology Handbook*, http://www.tenement.org/docs/interpmeth.pdf.
5. Ibid.
6. Wikipedia http://en.wikipedia.org/wiki/Native_American_name_controversy.
7. Amanda J. Cobb, "The National Museum of the American Indian as Cultural Sovereignty" in in *The National Museum of the American Indian Critical Conversations*, edited by Amy Lonetree and Amanda J. Cobb (Lincoln: University of Nebraska Press, 2008), 333.
8. Patricia Pierce Erikson, "Decolonizing the 'Nation's Attic' in Lonetree," *The National Museum of the American Indian Critical Conversations*, edited by Amy Lonetree and Amanda J. Cobb (Lincoln: University of Nebraska Press, 2008), 46.
9. David Hurst Thomas, *Skull Wars: Kennewick Man, Archaeology and the Battle for Native American Identity* (New York: Basic Books, 2000), 29.
10. Thomas, *Skull Wars*, 41
11. Thomas, *Skull Wars*, 92
12. Thomas, *Skull Wars*, 98

13. Kristina Ackley, "Tsiʔniyukwalihoʔta, the Oneida Nation Museum Creating a Space for Haudenosaunee Kinship and Identity" in *Contesting Knowledge Museums and Indigenous Perspectives*, edited by Susan Sleeper-Smith (Lincoln: University of Nebraska Press, 2009), 264.
14. Erikson, "Decolonizing the 'Nation's Attic,'" 73.
15. Ruth B. Phillips, "Why Not Tourist Art? Significant Silences in Native American Museum Representations" in *After Colonialism Imperial Histories and Postcolonial Displacements*, edited by Gyan Prakash (Princeton, NJ: Princeton University Press, 1994), 116.
16. Ackley, "Tsiʔniyukwalihoʔta," 264.
17. Cobb, "The National Museum of the American Indian as Cultural Sovereignty," 334.
18. Darby Stapp and Michael S. Burney, *Tribal Cultural Resource Management: The Full Circle to Stewardship* (Lanham, MD: AltaMira Press, 2002), 52.
19. Amy Lonetree, *Decolonizing Museums: Representing Native America in National and Tribal Museums* (Chapel Hill: University of North Carolina Press, 2012), 9.

Acknowledgments

This book is part of a larger series on interpreting in history museums, and I would like to thank Cinnamon Catlin-Legutko and Bob Beatty for thinking of me and giving me the opportunity to be part of it. I would also like to thank Charles Harmon, my editor, for his help, support, and suggestions along the way.

I sincerely acknowledge and thank each of the people who contributed a case study, interview, or other comments to the text. The collective wisdom and experience they represent is inspiring to me personally, and I hope for all who read this book. Each of the authors volunteered their time, expertise, and experiences to this process, which given the other responsibilities in their lives, is remarkable.

I am grateful to the many people I have worked with in the museum field over the years and who have all taught me elements of the profession that I take with me in my work. I have enjoyed learning how to improve interpretation and visitor experience from independent and seasoned museum professionals and from visitors and students. I appreciate the thorough education I received at the University of Nebraska–Lincoln in the Museum Studies Department and wish that program and the dedicated professionals who were part of it were still shaping new generations of museum professionals. I want to thank Mandy Langfald and Stacey Walsh for their ongoing support and guidance.

In addition, I have been fortunate to work with amazing Native advisors, colleagues, and friends from all over the country. Both within the museum profession, and working and socializing together outside of the museum world, I have learned more then I can say from many patient teachers. There are several to whom I am deeply thankful, including Anne Marie Sayers, my first teacher. The lessons I learned from working with her guide me every day to be open and kind and that "in breath as it is in spirit" are words worth living by. I would especially like to thank the five Native Nations of the Wabanaki—the Maliseet, Micmac, Passamaquoddy, Penobscot, and Abenaki. I am fortunate to count friends and teachers among each of these communities, and I have long relied on their honesty and openness to be successful in my work. Specifically, I would like to thank David Moses Bridges and George Neptune for always being available for any questions I might have or to discuss a nagging feeling in my gut about a program or idea. John Bear Mitchell, Maria Girouard, James Eric Francis, Sr., John Banks, Theresa Secord, Jennifer Neptune,

Donald Soctomah, Darren Ranco, Molly Neptune Parker, and Roger Paul have also provided invaluable support over the years. There are many others as well, who have guided me through this work with kindness and grace.

Finally, I would like to acknowledge that interpretation of Native culture is changing rapidly. There are new, amazing resources available all of the time, and great work is being done to consider the role of first-person voice and truth-telling in museums. This work is helping to transform museums from spaces about the "Other," to places for everyone to gather and learn together. It is a remarkable and enjoyable time to be part of this dynamic profession. The work of Amy Lonetree has been particularly helpful, as well as Ruth Phillips and others cited in this book. As long as the lessons of respect, communication, and honesty are incorporated into our daily work, hopefully the experiences shared in this book will provide a solid foundation on which new collaborations can flourish.

CHAPTER 1

Knowing the History

A Brief History of Federal Indian Policy

Introduction

One of the first and most important steps to accurately interpret Native history and culture, and to form partnerships with Native advisors and communities, is to understand history. This chapter will summarize a selection of critical treaties, acts of Congress, and court cases that define the status of Native Americans in the United States today.

Public education in the United States lacks a thorough and comprehensive survey of Native history. Rarely do textbooks maintain a thread of Indian history past settlement by Europeans and Americans, leaving the misconception that Indians either moved, perished, or assimilated into mainstream society. "Contact is tightly linked to an inevitable cultural decline leading toward a vanishing point around 1900. After this portentous date a silence falls, the stillness of death signifying the disappearance of the Indian that has been foretold in the text by the unremitting use of the past tense."[1]

Native people are not minorities struggling to find a way to integrate into American life. They are members of sovereign nations struggling in the face of ongoing oppression to maintain traditions and identity that stretch back millennia. Most Americans do not know the complexities and confusing history of American Indians. Museums are one place where new learning is possible. Author Amy Lonetree has been exploring how museums deal with difficult aspects of Indian history. She states that:

> In speaking the truth about the violence in our history, we are ensuring that future generations can never claim ignorance of this history. Desmond Tutu states, regarding the South African Truth and Reconciliation Commission, "No one in South Africa could ever again be able to say, 'I didn't know,' and hope to be believed."

Lonetree points out that museums should serve as sites where the hard truths of history between Native and non-Native colonists should be told honestly. "We need to make sure that our museums include the difficult stories that serve to challenge deeply embedded stereotypes—not just the ones of Native disappearance that museum presentations of the past have reinforced in the nation's consciousness, but the willed ignorance of this nation to face its colonialist past and present."[2] To ensure accurate interpretation, it is important to be familiar with some of the defining laws and events that continue to affect Native people

Early Relations between Indians and Europeans

Prior to European contact, American Indians populated almost all regions of the Americas. These indigenous communities had their own governments and social organizations. At the time of European contact, American Indian groups were sovereign—autonomous governments, free from external control.[3] With sovereignty comes a bundle of rights; the right to hunt and fish in one's own territory, the right to define citizenship, and the right to regulate internal affairs without foreign control or interference are just a few examples. Of the hundreds of American Indian nations living in what is now the United States, their political, social, and economic structures differed greatly and still do.

When European explorers started traveling to North America they met with these sovereign nations and understood that Native people had rights to the land and resources. The challenge was to find a way to divest native nations of those rights that would hold up under the scrutiny of other Europeans and international law.

In the fifteenth century, the Catholic Church issued a series of papal bulls (or decrees) that defined the process through which European nations could conquer other lands. In an effort to avoid conflict over land claims between European leaders, the decrees created standards by which competing European powers could understand one another's claims to newly discovered lands. The problem was, these lands were already inhabited.

In part, the Church stated that the "Christian Law of Nations" asserted a divine right to claim absolute title and authority over any newly discovered non-Christian lands and inhabitants. This belief gave rise to the Doctrine of Discovery, used by Spain, Portugal, England, France, and Holland as they claimed title to lands in North America. The doctrine claimed that no one owned non-Christian lands, and once a Christian monarch had claimed the right of dominion, that claim was transferred to any political successors. federal Indian policy is built on this concept, which was solidified by Chief Justice John Marshall and the Supreme Court in *Johnson v. M'Intosh* (1823).

The doctrine justified taking Native lands, but doing so required a legal process, and treaties became the process by which agreements were made between Europe, American Indian leaders, and later, the United States. Treaties are documents signed between nations agreeing to certain terms. Each nation enters treaty negotiations with a bundle of rights inherent in their sovereignty, and those rights are retained unless specifically signed away. If title over a sovereign is transferred, for example when the British relinquished title to the United States, existing treaty obligations are transferred to the new nation. Because of the treaty process, federally recognized Indian tribes have retained a degree of their sovereign status. It is important to understand that Indian nations do not have "special rights," and they have not been "given" land or this unique status. Indian nations have retained certain rights through fierce protection of cultural values and constant adaptation to the changing realities around them.

Europeans brought the treaty process, signing documents that outline the terms agreed on, to Native people, but the process of negotiating a treaty in North America became a Native construct.[4] Treaty negotiations with Native people involved much ceremony and often took several days that included speeches, gift-giving, and feasts. Early English records indicate frustration with how drawn out Native people made negotiations, and Europeans often misunderstood much of what was going on. Exchanging gifts was common practice, representing friendship, respect, and good faith in the process. Europeans, although gladly accepting gifts, rarely gave them in return or were disdainful of the process and had the opinion that by giving gifts Native people were acknowledging submission.[5]

Many Native communities were governed through consensus or democratic-like systems, requiring representatives at treaties to take conditions back to the community to discuss and approve or disapprove the conditions collectively. This was not a process that Europeans understood, and often participants left the negotiations drawing two different conclusions. Differences in cultural values and foundational understandings about land ownership and use also led to misunderstandings and conflict.

Early Relations between Indians and the United States

Federal Indian relations are complex, and consist of a long series of laws, court cases, and policies that alternate between self-determination and recognition of Indian sovereignty on the one hand, and paternalistic control and termination of trust status on the other. The following summary is by no means comprehensive, but rather highlights a few important court cases and federal laws that define Indian policy and status in the United States today. See appendix 1 for a timeline of important events in federal Indian relations.

In 1763, Britain issued the Royal Proclamation, which reserved the territory between the crest of the Appalachian Mountains and the Mississippi River for Indians. Settlers already living in this region were ordered to leave and further encroachment onto Indian lands was prohibited.[6] The proclamation also made it illegal for individuals to buy land directly from Indians, stating only the Crown could make land agreements with Indian delegations (reinforcing the nation-to-nation relationship between European and Indian sovereigns). The proclamation was abandoned soon after it was made, but it established several precedents for how the United States would later interact with Native people, including concepts of removal, reservations, and treaty negotiations.

After the formation of the United States, the new nation had to establish a system for regulating interaction with Native people living within and outside of the border. The US Constitution provided a strong central government, and "Indian relations, like foreign affairs, became the exclusive authority of the federal government."[7] Article III gave Congress the right to regulate trade with foreign nations and Indian tribes. In an effort to regulate trade, Congress passed the Trade and Intercourse Act in 1790, which was renewed every two years until a permanent Act was passed in 1802. The purpose of these acts was to separate Indians from non-Indians and subject all interaction between the two groups to federal control. The act regulated trade with Native people by forcing non-Natives to get a license from the federal government for any trade with Native people.

One of the most defining aspects of the acts was the establishment of a series of "factories," which were officially licensed trading posts where Native Americans could go to sell their merchandise. The factories were set up to protect the tribes from unscrupulous private traders; however, access to the factories could also be used as leverage to influence negotiations between the tribes and the United States. Because the increase of American settlers in the region was reducing access to traditional territories and available game for hunting, the factories were important to Native people to sell goods and purchase necessary foods, tools, and other items. Traders often used this as leverage to force the tribes to cede substantial territory in exchange for access to the factory.

The Marshall Trilogy

The right of the United States to regulate land acquisition with Native people was challenged in the Supreme Court in 1823 with *Johnson v. M'Intosh.* This is the first of three important Supreme Court rulings that combined define federal Indian law today. In this first case, two men, Johnson and M'Intosh, both acquired title to the same land—Johnson directly from an Indian tribe, and M'Intosh later acquired title to the same parcel of land from the federal government. Johnson argued that his title was superior to that of M'Intosh because he had bought the land directly from Native Americans. The district court disagreed, stating that the tribe never "owned" land in the legal sense of the word, and thus had no right to sell it. The Supreme Court was called on to decide whether the United States would recognize the power of Native Americans to give or sell land to private individuals, and implicitly, if Indians owned land, or merely occupied it.

Chief Justice Marshall ruled that based on the Doctrine of Discovery, European explorers (representing the rulers of Spain, France, Britain, Portugal, and others) gained free title to the lands they "discovered" and that the Native peoples living there had a right of occupancy (like renters). According to the court, Native people could not claim title to their lands because they did not believe in individual ownership and "productive use of the land."[8] Native people could sell their occupancy rights, but only to the discovering power, not to individuals or other nations. When England relinquished power, the United States inherited title, meaning Indians could only sell land to the US government.

By the mid-1800s, the population of the United States had grown dramatically, and so had its territory. New states were added to the union, many of which had large Indian populations living within the borders. In the southeast, several of the tribes understood the threat this meant to their sovereignty, and integrated aspects of American culture into tribal systems in an effort to be seen as "civilized" and therefore retain their sovereign status. The Cherokees, Chickasaw, Creeks, Seminoles, and Choctaws, which were known as the Five Civilized Tribes, adapted their governments to reflect that of the United States. The tribes created alphabets and written languages, published newspapers, and owned property that included large plantations and slaves. Americans living in the southeast, however, so desired Indian lands that no effort to imitate western culture would save the tribes from targeted destruction. In 1830, under growing pressure by states like Georgia, Andrew Jackson signed the Indian Removal Act. Although this act applied to tribes throughout the United States, it initially focused on southeastern tribes in Georgia, Alabama, Mississippi, and Florida.

The goal of Indian removal was to free up agricultural lands for white settlement and remove complications caused to states by having sovereign nations within the boundaries of that state. Native people were often seen as being in the way of progress, and removal was one way to clear large areas of land and resources for incoming settlers. As an incentive to move to newly designated land in the west called "Indian Territory" (present-day Oklahoma), the law provided financial and material assistance for Native people to travel to this new location and start new lives. The law also guaranteed that the Indians who had been removed would live on their new property (known as "reservations") under the protection of the US government forever. By the end of his presidency, Jackson had signed into law almost seventy removal treaties, the result of which was to move nearly fifty thousand eastern Indians to Indian Territory. Although much attention is placed on the Southeast and the removal of the Cherokees resulting in the Trail of Tears in 1838, many tribes were affected from all over the country—all with devastating loss of life and cultural upheaval.

In the midst of the removal, the Cherokee Nation was fighting to force the US government to recognize their sovereignty to protect themselves from aggressive intrusions from the state of Georgia into tribal affairs. When Georgia became a state, it gave up land in the west in exchange for a promise from the federal government that Indian title to lands would be extinguished. Getting impatient, Georgia began to divide up Cherokee land into counties and tried to extend state law onto tribal lands. Georgia also tried to make it illegal for the Cherokees to act as their own government. The Cherokee nation asked for an injunction, claiming that Georgia's state legislation had created laws, which, "go directly to annihilate the Cherokees as a political society."[9] In *Cherokee Nation v. Georgia* in 1831, the Cherokees argued that they were a foreign nation, recognized as such by the US constitution and laws, and therefore were not subject to Georgia's jurisdiction.

Chief Justice Marshall decided the case, which is the second in the three cases that create the foundation of modern federal Indian policy. Marshall ruled that the Cherokees were not a foreign nation, but were a "domestic dependent nation." Marshall was walking a fine line between the established relationship of the federal government and Indian tribes and the interests of the president, Jackson, who wanted the Cherokees removed from Georgia. Marshall was unwilling to leave the Cherokees at the mercy of the states, but he realized that the Cherokees could not function as a sovereign nation within the boundaries of the United States either. Instead, by labeling the tribes as "domestic dependent" he said they were not above the power of the United States and therefore could not sue as a foreign nation. This definition also left open the possibility of receiving federal protection against the states.

The Cherokees and their supporters knew that Marshall had left the door open to test the limits of what a domestic dependent nation might mean, and so a case was set up to send the Cherokees back to the Supreme Court in 1832. Georgia attempted to make non-Natives apply for a state permit to live or work on Indian lands. The Cherokees understood this to be in violation of their sovereignty so two missionaries moved onto Cherokee lands in violation of Georgia law and were arrested by the state. In *Worcester v. Georgia* (1832), Chief Justice

Marshall ruled again, stating that although the tribes were like wards to their guardian, this did not reduce their sovereignty. Marshall said that Indians have a protectorate relationship with the United States and that this protection did not imply the destruction of the protected. To summarize, Marshall decided that Indian nations were under the protection of the federal government, clarifying a direct federal–Indian relationship that did not involve states. In theory, this is the current political structure—federally recognized tribes have a direct relationship with the federal government, which does not include the states. More recent attempts to limit tribal sovereignty and state attempts at gaining control over Indian land has resulted in a complex web of relationships between tribes, states, and the federal government, making federal Indian law among the most complex in the world.

Western Territorial Expansion of the United States

Native people in the southwest began a complex relationship with the United State starting in 1848 when California, Nevada, Arizona, Utah, and parts of New Mexico, Colorado, and Wyoming were annexed by Mexico in the Treaty of Guadalupe Hidalgo. As part of the agreement, the United States assumed obligations to Indian nations made by Mexico, in which Indian communities enjoyed a degree of autonomy not found in the United States.

Prior to European contact, as today, there were many different cultural groups living in the southwest. Some were sedentary farmers, others were herders, and still other tribes were nomadic, following buffalo. Great environmental and cultural diversity resulted in areas of dense populations and other areas that were sparsely populated. The Spanish established a system of missions throughout the region in the 1700s, forcing Native people to convert to Christianity or face dire consequences. Even those who did convert faced harsh treatment at the hands of the Spaniards.

The Pueblo communities living along the Rio Grande in New Mexico and stretching into Arizona worked hard to retain their spiritual autonomy. The communities were isolated and independent, although there was strong Spanish influence and control exerted over Native governance and spiritual life. After repeated and targeted aggression against Pueblo spiritual leaders by local Spanish leaders, the tribes had enough and planned a revolt to remove the Spanish and Catholicism once and for all. In 1680 a plan was unleashed and the Pueblos successfully drove more than two thousand Spanish settlers from the region for twelve years. When the Spanish returned, they did so with a new respect for Pueblo rights and independence, and the tribes retained a high level of autonomy as a result. When Mexico gained independence from Spain, Native people became citizens of the new nation, and the Pueblo tribes retained a degree of political autonomy.

The Treaty of Guadalupe Hidalgo stipulated that the Pueblo tribes would remain independent and maintain ownership of their lands when the territory became part of the United States. Native people were not citizens of the Unites States at this time; however, the treaty granted citizenship to all southwestern Indians now living in the United States, which created a confusing parallel of rights and identity for Native people.

The United States also agreed not to remove any Indians from their traditional territories, as was being done to the southeastern tribes under Jackson's Indian Removal Act. As a result, most of the southwest tribes affected by the Treaty of Guadalupe Hidalgo remain in their homelands.

Assimilation-Era Policies and Reservations

In 1849 Indian affairs was moved from control of the War Department to the Department of the Interior, which marked a significant change in how Native rights and sovereignty were understood in the United States. Because they resided fully within the territorial boundaries of the United States and not on the frontier of western expansion, Indian nations were no longer considered foreign sovereigns. This shift in federal–Indian relations paved the way for the United States to cease treaty negotiations with Indian nations, which ended in 1868 when the last treaty was signed, making a total of 370 treaties signed between the United States and Indian nations. After this date, new federal policies affecting Indian people would come from Congress, not from treaty councils.

In addition to negotiating with the United States to retain political and cultural independence, Native people have faced challenges from other sources. The purpose of the Indian Removal Act was to separate Indians and whites, and in theory, allow each to live independently from one another. The reality was that white encroachment onto reserved Indian lands did not stop regardless of where the territorial boundaries lay. The United States wanted to "get out of the Indian business" and removal was not going to be enough. One of the unexpected drawbacks to the reservation system was that Indian culture could flourish in many of the same ways it always had. Communities retained traditional governments, language, communal ownership, political and ceremonial traditions and practices, and other aspects of cultural values.

By 1860 a series of day schools had been established near many reservations to educate Native youth in English and domestic skills in an effort to assimilate them into white society. Children went to school during the day, but they continued to live at home with their families. This allowed Native children to continue speaking their language and participating in cultural activities on the reservation, which slowed or prevented assimilation into white society. For many, this meant that the schools were failing to assimilate Indian children, which was one of their purposes.

In 1875 Army Lieutenant Richard Henry Pratt had an opportunity to experiment with a group of seventy-two Indian prisoners of war by removing them from the influences of their tribal communities and immersing them into a regimented educational program thousands of miles away from their tribal homelands. Pratt introduced classes in English, Christianity, art, guard duty, and craftsmanship, with the goal of teaching Native people the skills needed to become farmers or laborers.[10] His success in teaching the prisoners inspired him to create the Carlisle Indian Industrial School in Pennsylvania. He modeled it on military life, with students doing most of the domestic jobs required to run the school, including janitorial work, cooking, cleaning, and farming.

In the late 1800s, there was a debate taking place among politicians, religious leaders, and interested citizens about what to do with Native American populations. The establishment of the reservation system removed Indians from proximity to many white settlements; however, as the American population grew, demand for Indian lands grew too. One idea that gained popularity was to put an end to outright warfare against Indian cultures and focus on assimilating Native people into mainstream society. "If the Indians are to live at all, they must learn to live like white men. They can no longer stand in the way of the development of the country, but they must be enabled to become part of that development, and thus to be benefited by it."[11]

As a means of solving "the Indian problem," Pratt spoke with passion about the potential of assimilating Native people into American society through education and conversion to Christianity. "A great general has said that the only good Indian is a dead one, and that high sanction of his destruction has been an enormous factor in promoting Indian massacres. In a sense, I agree with the sentiment, but only in this: that all the Indian there is in the race should be dead. Kill the Indian in him, and save the man."[12] Carlisle became a model for a system of boarding schools across the United States and Canada, with the express purpose of removing Indian children from the influences of home and family, by sending them to distant schools.

The US government operated more than one hundred boarding schools, and somewhere between twenty and thirty thousand Native American children went through the system, which was often administered and staffed by Christian religious organizations. The schools were notorious for their brutality and strict discipline. Children were beaten if they spoke their language or were caught practicing tribal traditions. Many children suffered physical, sexual, and mental abuse at the schools. When the children returned to the reservations after graduation, many found it difficult to integrate themselves back into their families because they did not speak the same language or share the same traditions and values. The effects of these schools have been devastating, passing historical trauma on to many generations.

Since the first Trade and Intercourse Act was passed in 1790, the United States has limited tribal sovereignty and jurisdiction in numerous ways (many of which have been mentioned herein). In 1883, the Supreme Court recognized that tribal governments had legal authority over tribal members who committed crimes on tribal lands.[13] The Court ruled that Congress had not enacted legislation specifically limiting jurisdiction of Indian crimes on Indian lands and transferring that power to the United States. As a result, Congress passed the Major Crimes Act in 1885, which took jurisdiction away from the tribes for seven "major" crimes, and placed it in the hands of the US government. The list of crimes has since been expanded several times, and now consists of fifteen offenses. The Major Crimes Act has removed the inherent right of Native people to apply their own laws and systems of justice on their own lands.

The reservation system fell under attack again in 1887 with passage of the Dawes Severalty Act, or General Allotment Act. Because the reservations encouraged communal living and allowed for continuation of cultural values and religious practices, pressure mounted to break up the reservations and force Native people onto individual parcels of land that they would farm. The Dawes Act divided the reservations into parcels of land, the size of which was determined by the amount of Indian blood each individual could trace.[14] Indians who were full-blooded received 160 acres of land, half-blooded Indians received 80 acres of land, and so on, and after a transition period, in theory, held title outright. However, full-blooded Indians were often deemed "incompetent" to manage their own affairs and management of the land was given to government agents, who leased the lands to oil, ranching, and timber speculators.

Families were given parcels of land without roads, access to water, and oftentimes far apart from one another. Any "surplus" lands not divided among tribal members through the allotment process was opened for land grants and private sale, which is where the land in the Oklahoma land rush, and others, came from. Individuals who went through the allotment process also became citizens of the United States.

Citizenship and Tribal Reorganization

By 1924 there was a large population of Native people who were also citizens of the United States, through treaties, allotment, or other means. There were also Native people who had not been made citizens, and it was unclear what rights they did and did not have. To clarify and make Indian citizenship uniform, the Indian Citizenship Act was passed in 1924, giving all Indians full citizenship in the United States and the right to vote in federal elections for the first time.

For many reasons, the Dawes Act was a complete failure, leaving many Native people impoverished and dependent on government aid to survive. Poor distribution of allotments, unscrupulous land speculators, and poor management of leases all contributed, which led to a study of the condition of Indian people published in 1928.[15] The study called for an end to the Allotment Act and recognition of Indian people and sovereignty. In 1934, the Indian Reorganization Act was passed, ending the practice of allotment and reorganizing tribal lands that had gone through allotment back into reservations, albeit smaller than the original because of the land rushes. The Reorganization Act also recognized the sovereignty of tribal governments and created a process by which tribal governments could regain a level of autonomy. Tribal governments could reorganize under a structure that reflected that of the United States by voting for representatives and government officials, and adopting a constitution. Many tribes chose to reorganize under this act, but not all. Tribes who did not choose to reorganize expressed concern about abandoning traditional forms of government. This act remains an influential element of tribal sovereignty today and continues to define the federal Indian recognition process.[16]

The Termination Era and Erosion of Tribal Sovereignty

Federal Indian policy can be seen as a roller coaster, with "high" periods in which Indian people and governments are empowered to maintain traditions and values, and "lows" in which the US government enacted policies targeted at the destruction of Native culture and sovereignty. In 1953, the Termination Act started another low cycle with a devastating policy that removed the trust status for Indian lands. Indian rights were viewed as "special" rather than retained, and the United States wanted to end the federal–Indian relationship. It was argued (again) that Indians would be better off if they assimilated into mainstream society.

The Termination Act removed reservation lands from trust status and dissolved tribal governments and exemptions, exposing Indian people and businesses to state regulation. Tribes who had become economically self-sufficient and were operating successful tribal businesses were targeted first. One hundred and nine tribes were terminated between 1953 and 1975 before the policy was abandoned and finally repealed in 1988.

At the same time that the Termination Act was removing trust status for Indian lands and recognition of tribal status, Public Law 280 was passed. This law gave criminal and civil jurisdiction to certain states with large Indian populations on certain Indian reservations, but not all Indian reservations within the state. The tribes were not consulted in this process, and the five original states selected to participate were not granted funds to manage Indian affairs. Public Law 280 radically shifted the balance of jurisdictional power toward the states and away from federal and tribal governments, despite the ruling by the Supreme Court protecting tribes from states. The law does not alter the trust status of tribal land or terminate the relationship between tribes and the federal government, nor does it grant full jurisdiction to the participating states. It further confuses an already complex relationship between three types of governments—tribal, state, and federal.[17]

Self-Determination

In the 1970s, Native people battling inequality and fighting for the right to remain culturally and politically distinct began to see some progress. President Richard Nixon passed the Indian Self-Determination and Education Assistance Act in 1975. This act denounced termination and pledged federal resources "to strengthen the Indian's sense of autonomy without threatening his sense of community." The act allowed the secretaries of the interior and health and human services to contract directly with tribal governments to administer service programs, such as housing, health care, and education. It is also the foundation for later acts that require consultation with tribal governments before decisions affecting tribes can be made. The Self-Determination Act enabled tribal governments to manage their own housing, law enforcement, education, health care, social services, and community development programs reflective of tribal values and priorities.

Throughout their entire history with the United States, Indian people have been persecuted and punished for practicing their religion; Native people are the only group in the United States who has needed a specific act of Congress to protect their religious freedom. As a result of centuries of religious persecution, Congress passed the Native American Religious Freedom Act in 1978. The act recognizes that Native religious practices often require access to sacred sites, and that traditional objects, medicines, and practices which had been outlawed and forced underground needed to be protected. The success of this act has been limited because it is rarely upheld in courts. The act requires federal agencies that manage public lands to adjust policies to allow for religious practices, but this has not been done uniformly.

During this era of self-determination, scrutiny was placed on the boarding school policies of the past. Despite the fact that government-operated boarding schools fell out of favor in the mid-1900s, the practice of assimilating Indian youth as a means of eliminating Indian culture and sovereignty continued. In 1978, the Indian Child Welfare Act was passed to stop the practice of adopting Native children out of Indian families and placing them with white families. Indian governments received a stronger voice in the process of adoption, advocating placing children in need with tribal or extended families, which reflected cultural values more closely.

In 1988, Congress passed the Indian Gaming Regulatory Act in response to the rise of high-stakes gambling facilities opening on reservations. The act classified four types of gaming, and established a gaming commission to regulate the industry, making tribal gaming the most regulated in the world. Income from casinos and high-stakes bingo games fund education initiatives, including language and culture classes, as well as cultural centers, elder support, and other business ventures.

Most museum professionals are familiar with the Native American Graves Protection and Repatriation Act (NAGPRA). The act mandates that museums receiving federal funding are required to notify Indian tribes of human remains, funerary artifacts, and objects in collections pertaining to religious practices and cultural patrimony. Because there is a vast number of articles and books written about NAGPRA, it is not necessary to go into great detail here. That NAGPRA has fostered new partnerships and standards for museums and tribes is noteworthy, making this conversation about best practices for museums and tribes possible.

The Indian Arts and Crafts Act was passed as a truth-in-advertising law to limit the number of products being sold as "authentic Native" craft. This act specifically affects museum shops because it defines who can market and sell arts and crafts labeled as "Indian."

Recently, there have been several executive orders signed with the purpose of improving federal–Indian relations and restoring elements of sovereignty. In 2000, the Consultation and Coordination with Tribal Governments order was signed, "to establish regular and meaningful consultation and collaboration with tribal officials in the development of Federal policies that have tribal implications, to strengthen the United States government-to-government relationships with Indian tribes, and to reduce the imposition of unfunded mandates upon Indian tribes."[18]

In 2008, while running for president, Barack Obama promised to meet regularly with Indian leaders to strengthen the nation-to-nation relationship tribes have with the United States. As of 2012, Obama hosted four conferences, listening to Indian leaders discuss sovereignty, education, economic issues, and cultural concerns. In 2010, Obama issued the Tribal Law and Order Act, which strengthened tribal courts, increased protection and prevention of crime on Indian lands by improving training and communication for tribal and local law enforcement officers, and increased resources to protect Native women, who are statistically more likely to suffer physical and sexual abuse than non-native women. This act helps return a small degree of jurisdictional control to Indian law enforcement agencies and courts over people committing crimes on Indian lands.

The roller coaster of federal Indian policy seems to be on an upswing in some ways, but at the same time there are always new challenges. For museum professionals who want to develop a respectful, mutually beneficial relationship with Native nations, keeping up to date on tribal events, politics, and federal Indian policy is key to understanding what other concerns are facing the tribes. It is important to remember that museum deadlines and needs will often be secondary to that of the tribe.

There is a common assumption that American Indians are holding on to historical trauma and an antiquated sense of identity to the detriment of being able to assimilate into mainstream American values and lifestyle. A review of newspaper or Internet articles about mascots, cultural and religious appropriation, or tribal assertions of sovereignty will bring up countless examples of Indian people being told to "get over it." The question is, get over what? How can a community move forward and put the past behind them when the damage is ongoing? A quick search online for the term *Native American* provides ample evidence of how Native people are being forced to live in the past to retain their identities, and new pop culture stereotypes are popping up so fast it is impossible to keep up.

Museums are overwhelmingly identified as places of truth and accuracy, where Americans and visitors from abroad go to learn more about our collective history and identity, and where we are going in the future. That being the case, museums have the responsibility to understand how American Indians are understood in modern society and work to correct assumptions and misinformation. Exhibits and programs staff have the opportunity to work directly with Native and non-Native people to foster community and personal interactions that break through stereotypes and provide meaning and transformative experiences that will be shared with others. These relationships are more clearly understood, but museums have the opportunity and responsibility to go further and build partnerships that are institution-wide and not project based. This is where best practices will truly transform how we interpret and present Native history and culture in nontribal museums.

Notes

1. Ruth B. Phillips, "Why Not Tourist Art? Significant Silences in Native American Museum Representations," in *After Colonialism Imperial Histories and Postcolonial Displacements*, edited by Prakash Gyan (Princeton, NJ: Princeton University Press, 1994), 101.
2. Amy Lonetree, "Museums as Sites of Decolonization Truth Telling in National and Tribal Museums," in *Contesting Knowledge Museums and Indigenous Perspectives*, edited by Susan Sleeper-Smith (Lincoln: University of Nebraska Press, 2009), 326.
3. Merriam-Webster online.
4. Daniel K. Richter, *Facing East From Indian Country: A Native History of Early America* (Cambridge, Mass.: Harvard University Press, 2003).
5. Richter, *Facing East From Indian Country.*
6. Sharon O'Brien, *American Indian Tribal Governments* (Norman: University of Oklahoma Press 1989), 48.
7. O'Brien, *American Indian Tribal Governments*, 51.
8. O'Brien, *American Indian Tribal Governments*, 213.
9. O'Brien, *American Indian Tribal Governments*, 57.
10. http://en.wikipedia.org/wiki/Richard_Henry_Pratt.
11. Carl Schurz, "Aspects of the Indian Problem," *The American Missionary*, April 1883, 37, no. 4:105–107.
12. Richard Henry Pratt, "The Advantages of Mingling Indians with Whites" in *Americanizing the American Indians: Writings by the "Friends of the Indian" 1880–1900* (Cambridge, Mass. Harvard University Press, 1973), 260–271.
13. *Ex parte Crow Dog* involved a case in which an Indian man was murdered on Indian lands and the tribe resolved the crime working within traditional structures. Non-Native friends of the

victim were outraged that the murderer was not brought to trial and demanded he be hanged. The case went before the Supreme Court.

14. This is the foundation for the current method of quantifying how much Indian blood (or ancestry) an individual has in order to prove their identity and claim citizenship with an Indian Nation. The practice is known as "blood quantum."
15. *The Problem of Indian Administration*, also known as the Meriam Report, cited poor health, short life spans, and crippling poverty for Indian people living on reservations or allotment lands.
16. Federal recognition is the legal process a tribe goes through to be acknowledged as a sovereign nation by the United States. Tribes must be able to prove they have operated a continuous government, among other things, to gain recognition. The Indian Reorganization Act comes into play during this process as well and is currently under fire for its limitations in respecting traditional forms of government.
17. Public Law 280 has lost some of its strength because of a backlash from tribes arguing that they were not consulted. Now tribes and states must negotiate to participate in Public Law 280, to which no tribe has voluntarily agreed.
18. Excerpt from signing statement by Bill Clinton; for full statement and law, see http://www.gpo.gov/fdsys/pkg/WCPD-2000-11-13/pdf/WCPD-2000-11-13-Pg2806-2.pdf.

CHAPTER 2

Getting Started

RELATIONSHIPS are based on trust. Native American tribes have a long and complicated relationship with museums in the United States, and museum staff will need patience and consistency to build or repair relationships with the Native communities represented in their collections. This chapter outlines steps that can be taken to begin new relationships or repair damaged, outdated relationships between museums and tribal communities.

The First Step: Which Tribes Does the Museum Represent?

Before museum staff can start building relationships, strengthen existing relationships, or repair damaged relationships with Native people, they need to take a critical look at which tribes are represented by the museum, both in collections, but also in the wider community, region, and museum audience. Take some time to research who the tribes are, and who the tribes were, and challenge any assumptions that staff and stakeholders already know this information. In the Southeast, Great Plains, and other places in the United States, Native communities were removed to another part of the country as part of a federally mandated and systematic effort to separate Native and non-Native populations. In almost all removal histories, there are portions of the population who stayed behind, hiding in rural areas or in plain sight by suppressing their identity.

Museums that are located in regions where tribes were removed will need to consider when and how to reach out to those removed communities and start building a relationship. They will need to seek advice from multiple parties about how best to integrate stories and build relationships with both the removed tribes and those tribal communities that remained. The relationships between removed tribes and members who remained behind can be strained at times, so be respectful of all points of view. Museums have the potential to reconnect removed tribes with collections and stories from their home territory and can become a platform for direct Native voice about their experiences, world view, and relationship to place—both before and after removal.

In addition to removal, most tribes suffered huge population loss as a result of disease and warfare. At times, survivors from these communities integrated into other tribes as refugees. Each region of the country has a different history with Native people, and each tribe has a unique history of survival strategies that have carried them through to today. Be sensitive to this legacy and respect the hard decisions tribal members and leaders have had to make, and continue to make, as their communities move into the future.

During this initial research phase, museum staff will also need to determine if there are nonfederally recognized tribes represented in the region or in the collections. There are four legal classifications that define tribal status in the United States:

1. Federally recognized tribes: These tribes maintain a political relationship with the federal government, usually established by treaty or congressional legislation. There are more than 565 federally recognized tribes in the United States.[1]
2. State recognized tribes: Tribes recognized by the state in which they live as being a unique cultural and political entity from the state. The federal government does not recognize the political sovereignty of these tribes.
3. Terminated tribes: These are tribes whose federal trust status was terminated during the Termination Act of the 1950s and whose tribal status has not been reaffirmed.
4. Unrecognized tribes: These tribes have no political relationship with the federal or state governments. They have no tribal lands.[2]

Federal recognition is controversial in many ways because it is not a Native construct, but one that tribes have been forced to adopt so they can maintain sovereign status and a direct government-to-government relationship with the United States. Because federal recognition means that tribes with this status have access to services incurred by the federal government though treaty—and it is understood that these services are limited—there can be an instinct to protect those obligations; meaning there is little incentive by both the federal government and tribes to recognize more nations.

But it is not only an economic concern. Federal recognition represents an acknowledgement of continuous tribal identity and governance that has been maintained against all odds, and at high costs to life, community values, language, and religious traditions. Tribal nations who have maintained cultural continuity are naturally protective of the integrity of this process and status. On the other hand, both tribes and people working with tribes understand that the legacy of violent and assimilation policies in the United States means that not all tribes can prove a continuous functioning government, and if they have a sense of identity and cultural continuity at all, it is success against the odds. To ignore this history and complexity and simply work with federally recognized tribes risks subscribing to a legacy of colonial domination that undermines true collaborations. Each museum will need to consider the history of the tribes from their region, identify the federally and any nonfederally recognized tribes, and come to a determination about how to balance these concerns.

Outcomes for this initial research phase include:

- Identify the names and status of all tribes represented by the museum in terms of collections and region.

- Discuss the process for working with federally recognized tribes, removed tribes, or tribes without federal recognition. Is it the same process, or will it vary to some degree?
- Locate where each tribe is located on a map, keeping in mind there may be more than one community (both in the region in which the museum is located but also in the case of removed tribes.)

Identify people and positions within the tribe that are the first points of contact. List the tribal leadership, and elected positions within the tribe that are likely to be project partners (elected officials include tribal chief[3] and council), Tribal Historic Preservation Officer (THPO), museum director if the tribe has a museum or cultural center, and if the tribe employs a tribal historian or has a cultural or historic preservation department.

Who are the other cultural leaders from the community? There are a couple of layers of people within the tribe to start conversations with. Elected officials and tribal employees (listed previously) are the first, official point of contact between museum staff and the tribe, but there are other cultural and linguistic leaders who are respected in the tribe for their knowledge and experience as culture keepers. Sometimes they have good relations with tribal leadership, and other times there may be factions that disagree. It is important to develop relations with as many people as you can—both elected officials and cultural leaders identified by the community. Anthropologist James Clifford notes that:

> Tradition-bearer status is more closely linked with the politics of heritage, and it can include people of more or less mixed background who in recent decades have returned to Native tradition, reactivating old crafts, languages, stories, and lifeways. It thus denotes an active commitment to transmitting community values and knowledge and recognizes the translation and education functions of individuals mediating between (deeply knowledgeable) elders and (relatively ignorant) youth. Its emergence is evidence that heritage activism extends beyond the goal of simply salvaging endangered lore.[4]

Become comfortable with multiple perspectives, and sometimes, conflicting perspectives. There is not one way to know about the past, but many lenses through which we can look to understand a story or object.

> There is no such entity as the Native voice, one that speaks with authority for the entire community. There exist many voices, some of which speak for upholders of cultural traditions, others that address band and tribal politics, and still others that concern themselves with social issues. . . . The encounters of different values, different priorities, often creates problems that can only sometimes be resolved.[5]

The Next Step: Look Inward

Once the initial research phase has been started and the staff has an understanding of who the tribes are, the next step is to conduct an internal audit of the museum's relationship, collecting practices, and history with the tribe(s). This can be a challenging, and sometimes emotional process; however, it is a vital step in establishing equal relations with the tribes in the future. Museum staff and board members must acknowledge the history of the museum, and each individual must spend some time thinking about his or her own assumptions, stereotypes, and expectations for working with Native people.[6]

After looking inward at assumptions and stereotypes within the board and staff, the same lens can be used to evaluate exhibits and interpretation. It is common practice now to involve Native people in the interpretation of tribal objects and history, but this is a relatively recent practice (within the last twenty years or so). Older museum exhibits often served to reinforce a dominant narrative of the "vanishing Indian," and even some modern exhibits continue to interpret this same perspective. Exhibits that include Native voice can be more representative of Native perspective, but only when presented with equal weight and integration to other sources of information. When looking at past and present exhibits, museum staff should consider the perspective presented to the public, question the messages of the text, and look for clues as to whether the interpretation serves to reinforce stereotypes of Native people.

> Western museums are a powerful colonizing force. . . .Western museum exhibits typically exoticize and distance the visitor from Indigenous people, placing the Native irrevocably in the past. In this view, the Indian was what the white man was not, the polar opposite of how white Americans defined themselves. U.S. museums added legitimacy to these cultural values even as they disseminated them, and are an important tool in upholding ideas about the exotic other.[7]

It can be argued that this process of self-reflection and evaluation is never over, but is ongoing, including training for new staff and board members, and informing new relationships with tribal people. With that in mind, once this process is underway, the next step is reaching out to tribal communities, whether within the structure of existing tribal relations or to form new relationships.

Reaching Out to Tribes

"Initially, rather than invite individual representatives of Native communities to travel to New York City or Washington, DC, the National Museum of the American Indian staff chose to travel to Native communities."[8] The importance of allowing time and budgeting for travel to the reservations or tribal communities cannot be overestimated. Museum staff can and should invite Native advisors to the museum for meetings, which for certain projects or phases within a project, is appropriate; but initially and periodically, it is important to spend time in tribal communities. There are many reasons why this is an important aspect of building relationships with Native nations. First, it allows the tribes to set the agenda for what they want to talk about and share with museum staff. Museum staff get invaluable insight into the projects, opportunities, values, and challenges faced by the community. Projects that tribal members would not think to share in the museum setting will more likely be shared when on the reservation. However, do not show up unexpected, uninvited, or without working with tribal advisors to first establish the goals for the meetings.

Often tribes are simultaneously working on many projects. As governments they are concerned with tribal businesses, environmental management projects, health and education improvements, and all other responsibilities of a governing body. In addition, tribes may also be focused on issues of language retention, cultural or religious appropriations, hunting and fishing rights, or internal tribal matters. Although many tribes understand that collaborations with outside educational organizations can be a means of improving understanding about tribal people and history, this may not be a priority for the tribe at that time. Do not get discouraged and give up! Patience and understanding will eventually lead to successful partnerships, or connect museum staff to tribal members who are able and willing to collaborate.

Before traveling to a reservation, take some time to find out more about tribal customs. Each tribe has different systems and cultural norms for working with non-Native people. Do not be shy about asking for information about expressions of respect and cultural norms expected of visitors, but ask in a respectful manner, and understand that there are limitations to the kinds of information available to people from outside of the tribe. Native communities are living cultures and when one travels into their territory it is customary to acknowledge and respect their unique customs.

Think about ways to give back or invest in the community. Consider bringing other members of the staff along on the visit, specifically the buyer for the museum store. The community can announce to local artists that the museum will be on the reservation buying from artists at a certain location and time. This process will introduce museum staff to new artists who may be interested in demonstrating their work at the museum, who want to collaborate on exhibits, and whose pieces could be added to the collection.

A Passamaquoddy storyteller, Roger Paul, once cautioned "leave your assumptions about us behind. You have never met anything like us before. Be open to what we want to share with you, and appreciate our history with new eyes."[9]

Ideally, the initial visits are not project driven but are relationship building. Work with the list of tribal people identified in the initial research phase and contact one or more to make appointments for a visit. Make it clear who you are and the purpose of the visit. The most logical points of contact are tribal museum or cultural center staff. The THPO or tribal historians are also good people to build relationships with. There are many ways to initiate conversations and build relations between tribal members and museum staff. For these early visits together, museum staff might ask if there are items in the collections that tribal members are interested in seeing. Bring these to the reservation, or at least photographs, collecting data, and any other information that might be helpful, and leave that information with the tribe. Transparency in the collections and museum policies will be important for establishing trust. Museum staff might also share the results of their internal audit on past interpretation and staff assumptions and ask for feedback about the findings and process. Taking ownership and responsibility for any past mistakes will help build trust. Ask if tribal members are comfortable sharing their experiences with the museum, and be sure to honor their perspectives and experiences. Ask if tribal members come to the museum in their free time, and find out why or why not. The first visits to the reservation should be focused on listening, not defenses of past museum practices. Really focus on hearing what the tribal members have to say and how they envision the future of the partnership.

Authority Sharing

When all parties are ready to move ahead with a project, it is important to build an equal relationship from the beginning.

> Research increasingly calls for explicit contract agreements and negotiated reciprocities. . . . Gone are the days when cultural anthropologists could, without contradiction, present "the Native point of view," when archaeologists and physical anthropologists excavated tribal remains without local permission, when linguists collected data on indigenous languages without feeling pressure to return the results in accessible form.[10]

Ask up front what the fees or honorariums are for Native advisors, and budget that into the project at the beginning.

Try not to approach tribal advisors with an exhibit or project plan already developed. An idea or draft outline will help guide the conversation and make clear what the museum needs from tribal consultants, but tribal consultants need the authority to guide the content of the project from the beginning. In development of exhibits at the Museum of the American Indian in Washington, D.C., "the collaborative nature of the effort transformed the project from one perceived as an 'infringement' upon intellectual property rights to one perceived as 'honoring' the tribe and building positive relations."[11]

Build in extra time for projects to allow tribal advisors to create, review, and edit everything representing their communities. Understand that tribes might also say no to a project, for a wide variety of reasons. Learn from the process, ask for feedback, and continue to communicate. "Local communities need to be able to say no, unambiguously, as a precondition for negotiating more equitable and respectful collaborations."[12]

Authority sharing is the process by which cultural leaders, curators, academics, historians, and exhibit staff all have equal weight in the development of the content for an exhibit, program, or policy. The team is developed with an eye toward bringing diverse perspectives and backgrounds to the table, each with his or her expertise, allowing the flow of information and ideas to shape the project. Traditionally, when Native advisors were included in this process, oral histories and personal narratives were not given equal weight to academic theory and perspectives from outside of the tribe.

"For generations, Native knowledge structures have been marginalized relative to official versions of knowledge. This does not necessarily mean that these subjugated knowledge's remain marginalized, however. On the contrary, Native American community museums have proven themselves to be innovative centers that attempt to infuse alternative ways of knowing into a public sphere."[13] Illustrating this point, museum critics such as Edward Rothstein have commented that "narratives told in tribal voices get in the way of scholarship or meaning," demonstrating that he does not consider Native bodies of knowledge valid or equal to Western bodies of knowledge.[14]

On the other hand, anthropologists Aron Crowell and Sonja Luhrmann point out that "listening to (Native) people about how they view their own history is equally important. There are times when the indigenous viewpoint is dramatically opposed to that of Western scholarship. The age-old question 'what is truth?' may be appropriate in this circumstance.

The proposition that there can be more then one truth is often overlooked."[15] To help all parties understand why authority sharing is important, one can point out that this is an opportunity to focus on respect, rather than agreement.

Kristina Ackley argues that "It has been very difficult to change this representation of Indigenous people in museums that are controlled by non-Natives. . . . Museum practices may incorporate such new techniques as shared curatorial practices with Indigenous people. Although the authority of museums has been contested as a result of this critique and shared practices, many tribes found that even if they had positive relationships with the non-Native staff of museums, they still were in an unequal power relationship that contributed to the continued dispossession of their people."[16]

A key to authority sharing is to recognize that there are multiple ways of learning about the past, including oral history, Native language, material culture, archaeology, primary source materials, and academic publications. Each has strengths and weaknesses, but taken together, a more complete story of the past can be created. For Native people, oral traditions are a vital part of their ongoing cultural uniqueness. "For generations and in countless museums even today, tribal origin stories have not been privileged, and if they are mentioned, museums present them as quaint myths of primitive peoples. . . . When museum professionals were faced with presenting sensitive topics, especially those of a more controversial nature, they would present a range of perspectives and leave it to visitors to weigh and value each."[17] That oral traditions have at times been mocked or underappreciated by non-Native people is a part of the museum past that needs to be addressed. "As Indigenous peoples, we have long established that we have a different way of understanding history than non-Native people, the most important difference being our adherence to the oral tradition."[18]

The rich depth of multiple narratives and perspectives working together to tell a story can help visitors better understand our shared histories. In his remarks at the opening of the George Gustav Heye Center in 1994, founding director, Rick West, Jr., said "I believe that these distinct ways of understanding are stated most articulately and are discerned by museum visitors most clearly when the Native voice is permitted, from an interpretive standpoint, to speak for itself."[19]

There are different ways in which project teams can work with Native advisors. Author Ruth Phillips distinguishes two basic models. "In the 'community-based' exhibition, indigenous authorities determine the selection and interpretation of materials. Museum curators function as facilitators, and a unified Native perspective is the goal. . . . The second, 'multivocal' model juxtaposes Native and non-Native perspectives. The goal is to display different interpretations of the same event or text based on a negotiation of shared authority between the participants."[20]

Conclusion

Whether starting new, resurrecting, or repairing damaged relations with Native people, it is important to remember that each tribal nation is different, and individuals within each tribe are different. Creating sustaining relationships with tribes will be an ongoing effort that includes institutional evaluation and review, staff and board training, and learning how to work outside of the comfort zone of museum educators, curators, collections staff, and leaders. The increased effort may seem daunting at times, but it is important to remember that Native communities are sovereign nations, not minority groups who have moved into the area. As a result, interpreting Native history is different. Wrapped into the fabric of local history are unique material culture, values, and languages that are markers on the landscape. Many tribes value working with non-Native partners for a variety of reasons, but there are pitfalls to be aware of. Learning as much about Native history and current events, and taking those things into account when building relationships, will be valuable to the process.

> Of course, such projects are only one aspect of indigenous self-determination politics today. Heritage is not a substitute for land claims, struggles over subsistence rights, development, educational, and health projects, defense of sacred sites, and repatriation of human remains and stolen artifacts, but it is closely connected to all these struggles. What counts as "tradition" is never politically neutral, and the work of cultural retrieval, display, and performance plays a necessary role in current movements around identity and recognition. . . . Heritage can be a form of self-marketing, responding to the demands of a multicultural political economy that contains and manages inequalities.[21]

Notes

1. Department of the Interior http://www.doi.gov/tribes/index.cfm.
2. Sharon O'Brien, *American Indian Tribal Governments* (Norman: University of Oklahoma Press, 1989), 90.
3. I use this term here because it is commonly used within tribes as title for the head elected official, but many tribes use other terms, sometimes referring to this position as governor or a traditional term. As part of the research, find out what this position is called, and use the appropriate term for each community.
4. James Clifford, "Looking Several Ways: Anthropology and Native Heritage in Alaska," *Current Anthropology* 45, no. 1 (February 2004): 15.
5. Clifford, "Looking Several Ways," 15.
6. Appendix 2 is an activity that staff and board can do to help facilitate identification and discussion about stereotypes.
7. Kristina Ackley, "Tsiʔniyukwalihoʔta, the Oneida Nation Museum Creating a Space for Haudenosaunee Kinship and Identity" in *Contesting Knowledge: Museums and Indigenous Perspectives*, edited by Susan Sleeper-Smith (Lincoln: University of Nebraska Press, 2009), 263.
8. Amanda J. Cobb, "The National Museum of the American Indian as Cultural Sovereignty" in *The National Museum of the American Indian Critical Conversations*, edited by Amy Lonetree and Amanda J. Cobb (Lincoln: University of Nebraska Press, 2008), 336.
9. Paul, Roger, Abbe museum presentation May 2012.
10. Clifford, "Looking Several Ways," 5.
11. Patricia Erikson, "Decolonizing the 'Nation's Attic'," *The National Museum of the American Indian: Critical Conversations*, edited by Amy Lonetree and Amanda J. Cobb (Lincoln: University of Nebraska Press, 2008), 55.

12. Clifford, "Looking Several Ways," 6.
13. Erikson, "Decolonizing the "'Nation's Attic,'" 45.
14. Cobb, "The National Museum of the American Indian as Cultural Sovereignty," 348.
15. Clifford, "Looking Several Ways," 19.
16. Ackley, "Tsiʔniyukwalihoʔta," 265.
17. Amy Lonetree, *Decolonizing Museums: Representing Native America in National and Tribal Museums* (Chapel Hill: University of North Carolina Press, 2012), 169–170.
18. Amy Lonetree, "Museums as Sites of Decolonization Truth Telling in National and Tribal Museums" in *Contesting Knowledge: Museums and Indigenous Perspectives*, edited by Susan Sleeper-Smith (Lincoln: University of Nebraska Press 2009), 328.
19. Erikson, "Decolonizing the 'Nation's Attic,'" 68.
20. Clifford, "Looking Several Ways," 21.
21. Clifford, "Looking Several Ways," 8.

CHAPTER 3

Consultation with Tribes and Advice from the Field

Citizen Potawatomi Nation Cultural Heritage Center

Kelli Mosteller, PhD, Director,
and R. Blake Norton, Archivist/Curator

IN 2005, with the approval of the Citizen Potawatomi Nation executive branch and tribal legislature, construction began on a 36,000-square-foot structure to serve as the hub of cultural preservation and education for the tribe. In January 2006, the Cultural Heritage Center in Shawnee, Oklahoma, opened to educate almost 30,000 tribal members and the public on the historical and contemporary aspects of the tribe through the acquisition, preservation, and exhibition of the diverse materials pertaining to the culture and traditions of the Citizen Potawatomi Nation (Figure 3.1). The Citizen Potawatomi Nation Cultural Heritage Center (Heritage Center) receives an estimated 7,000 visitors a year and is the site of many cultural activities hosted by the nation. The Heritage Center contains a classroom where weekly instruction is held in language, beading, regalia making, wood carving, and drawing. Classes such as making moccasins, drums, and baskets and ceremonial events are also hosted at the Heritage Center.

Serving as a living center for education, not only to our tribal membership but to the public at large, we are tasked with defining what makes the Citizen Potawatomi unique among the more than 566 recognized and unrecognized Native communities within the United States (Figure 3.2). Such an assignment necessitates a stratified approach that introduces visitors to the larger ***Neshnabek*** (Potawatomi, Odawa, and Ojibwe) cultural body and then narrows the focus to exclusively encompass Potawatomi characteristics, until finally examining the intricate tribal history and contemporary social presence of the Citizen Potawatomi.

Figure 3.1. Student participates in basket weaving class held in the Citizen Potawatomi Nation Cultural Heritage Center classroom. *Source:* Citizen Potawatomi Nation

From origin stories and lifeways to removal and allotments, varied topics of culture and history are necessary to paint a cohesive and true image of a sovereign Native nation.

The facility houses the Tribal Enrollment, Language, and Cultural Resources departments, the last of which includes the Archives and Research, Collections, and Tribal Heritage Productions programs and the library (Figure 3.3). The Archive and Research division works in concert with Tribal Enrollment to develop and maintain a systematic program for tracing genealogical lineage within the tribe. The Tribal Heritage Productions program advances the Heritage Center's goal of preserving Citizen Potawatomi history by conducting interviews with local tribal members and those who live throughout the United States. All of these programs, and the materials they preserve and produce, are used by the Heritage Center staff to create exhibits about Citizen Potawatomi lifeways, history, and culture in

Figure 3.2. Citizen Potawtaomi Nation Cultural Heritage Center. *Source:* Citizen Potawatomi Nation

our 16,000-square-foot gallery space.

Each of these departments is staffed by well-trained employees who have years of experience in their field. Since the Cultural Heritage Center opened, the museum staff, which consists of a director, curator, collections manager, and several other ancillary staff, have had numerous opportunities to partner with other institutions, both tribal and non-Native, on projects ranging from straightforward consultation to more involved collaborations to develop exhibits.

Figure 3.3. Archival collections housed in the Cultural Heritage Center's secure storage facility. *Source:* Citizen Potawatomi Nation

Making Contact

The process of consulting with a tribe will vary depending on the tribe(s) involved and the nature of the project. When beginning a new project, or seeking consultation from a tribe, the most important step is to establish a relationship with a key individual or group from the community. This person or group can help make the proper introductions and guide you through the proper process for working with officials and members of the tribe(s) and help establish meetings with the appropriate tribal partners. These initial meetings should be used to present the basic idea of the proposed collaboration and assess whether or not the tribe has any interest in being involved. If the tribal representatives make it clear that they do not want to participate, the museum team should reevaluate whether the project should continue. If the tribe does express a desire to work on the project, the museum staff can then start to work with the team to research what resources will be needed, what the role of tribal staff might be, and identify other contacts that may be needed. They should also develop a fundamental understanding of the basic customs and history of that tribe.

If a tribe has a cultural center or museum, this is a logical place for museum staff to make initial contact, which can potentially develop into a meaningful relationship and foster successful collaborations with the larger tribal community. Like those at the Heritage Center, the staffs of tribal museums and cultural centers are trusted by their nation to maintain and care for the objects in the tribe's collection and to portray the narrative the tribe chooses to present to the public. These employees are natural liaisons and can help facilitate productive partnerships. Though they will have a great deal of knowledge in the area of the tribe's history and culture, these individuals should be the first in a long line of contacts made within the community. The director or curator of a cultural center should be able to identify other vital contacts, which can include tribal administration, a cultural council, respected elders, or members of an individual family.

This is the case for the Heritage Center. We work to present cultural and historic knowledge and are familiar with the necessary protocol for our tribe. We know when we are free to make a decision, and when we need to consult elected officials, including the Cultural Committee within our legislative branch. We also know when exhibit ideas and subject matter should not be broached.

If a tribe does not have a cultural center with a director or a curator, the next point of contact is the tribe's elected officials, who can help identify the right people in the community to be contacted. Tribal members voted for these individuals to oversee the operations of the nation and their authority and position should be respected. The process of setting up meetings, making proper introductions, and following cultural customs can take a great deal of time, so consultation should be initiated as early as possible, and project timelines created with this in mind.

It is important that the person in charge of the final product be one of the individuals to make initial contact with the tribe. There needs to be a genuine interest in both hearing and implementing the thoughts and concerns of tribal members. Sincerity and dedication will be appreciated when building the relationship between outside museum staff and tribal members.

Working with a Sovereign Nation

Museum staff working with a Native population should be aware that there are long histories of intertribal and intratribal politics that may shape how they need to approach the consultation process. Ultimately, it is most important that the museum staff recognize that both tribal leadership and individual tribal members have a vested interest in how the community is portrayed. These individuals will often require final say in what information should be made public and what should not.

The most common collaborations happen when a nontribal museum wants to create an exhibit about a tribe, and the outside museum wants to engage more deeply with a specific population or group within the tribe. Many communities have subset groups that may have a different perspective on tribal history and culture or have had a different historical experience. This could include individuals from certain generations (i.e., elders or youth), spiritualists, elected officials, tribal members whose clan association gives them particular cultural roles, among many others. Their knowledge, life experience, or social status can lend a unique perspective to a project. Exhibit developers should be careful to differentiate between individual opinions, statements, and knowledge from the official or elected representation of the tribe.

There is great variation in tribal community structures, some of which could be cases of disparate groups that fall under one political entity and have divided over issues of culture or geography, but there are other tribes who are wholly divided and have separate political structures. Each group likely has a unique knowledge base, and reaching out to all groups will give the museum staff a better understanding of the community as a whole. Even if the groups do not have equal representation in an exhibition, equal weight ought to be given to the various experiences and opinions during the development stage.

When working on a project that includes a federally recognized tribe and additional subset groups that are not federally recognized, outside museum staffs need to be explicit in the distinction of the two groups. Both groups need to know up front that the perspective of the other will be included. This may change one group's willingness to participate, but it is important to build trust by being honest about the intentions and proposed final project from the beginning. Things such as tribal seals and other identifiers of a sovereign nation need to be used exclusively for the group they represent.

Cultural Considerations

Many soured relationships between tribes and non-Native institutions likely began on projects with the best of intentions. It is safe to assume that most of today's museum professionals are educated on the more inflammatory and damaging history between museums and tribes and want to create a productive and healthy working relationship. Some partnerships or relationships between Native and non-Native collaborations never truly develop, or collapse altogether, because museum staff lack sufficient knowledge or respect for tribal customs and sensitive topics, fail to adhere to cultural norms, or take a generalized, pan-Indian[1] approach to Native American subject matter.

Tradition and culture are threads that should weave throughout all interaction between museum staff and the Native peoples they are working with. To respect this, it is important to remember that gifting is a central cultural practice in many Native communities. It may be appropriate to bring gifts, offer tobacco or another medicine, or prepare a meal for an elder or someone from whom you wish to gain knowledge or teachings. Adhering to this practice will help the museum staff gain balance and understanding with the Native community. The tribal liaison for the project should be able to share what is culturally appropriate.

Collaborations may be a source of pride and celebration for a tribal community. For example, the Sac & Fox Nation hosted a feast to celebrate the collaboration between them, the Citizen Potawatomi Nation, and the staff of a local, non-Native museum in Oklahoma City. Members of the Sac & Fox Nation prepared a meal for all participants, a local drum group sang several songs, dancers performed, and tribal officials honored the group by speaking at the event. It was essential for the health of the relationship that everyone involved take the time to honor the agreement and successes in a good way.

Cultural constraints may be placed on museum staff and members of the tribal community in regard to the collection, and awareness and respect for this will be important to build successful partnerships. To holistically preserve and manage our ethnographic collections, the Heritage Center's curatorial and collections staff adhere to practices we have coined *Traditional Conservation*. These are culturally sensitive protocols combined with institutionally standardized practices, which allow for the implementation of a more holistic and respectful collections management program for American Indian collections. Collections comprised of spiritual, ceremonial or mortuary objects, or objects that are gender specific are believed to be created with a purpose, and contain a *mnedo* (spirit) that necessitates certain constraints. Other assemblages may require tribute in the form of food, water, or song, and highly restricted collections may require isolation or stipulate that the objects are conversed with in the parent language. Such beliefs and practices vary among tribes and may be contrary to programs within non-Native repositories because of their unconventionality and infringement on equal opportunity employment practices. Institutions housing collections of this nature usually contract with recognized spiritualists, elders, or knowledgeable members of the community to assist with object management.

Repairing or Building New Relationships with Tribes

When working with a tribe that has had negative experiences with museums in the past, outside museums must be willing to approach the new relationship with open-mindedness and a spirit of cultural humility. If possible, the museum staff should research what happened that ruined previous collaborative efforts. Knowing the nature of past experiences will help new partnerships avoid the same pitfalls and perhaps heighten awareness of other potential pitfalls.

It is also important to be honest if you as an individual, or the institution you represent, do not have a lot of experience working with Native Americans. Understand that the tribe could also be hesitant to work with a museum because they do not know what to expect. In cases such as these, both parties should work together to make sure that everyone's concerns, questions, and needs are being addressed.

One of the primary complaints that tribes have with museums is that they do not feel like they are equal partners in project development. The tribe must feel that the information and consultation they provide will be respected and taken to heart. They must have control over what information is and is not presented to the public, even if it is ultimately the responsibility of the museum staff to decide *how* that information is presented.

A tribal representative will have the expertise necessary to identify knowledge and teachings that are not to be shared with the public or items that should not be on display. Representatives may also have specific instructions about how an item should be properly displayed, and this information should not be disregarded. The tribe's wishes regarding what, where, and how objects and materials are exhibited should be respected. In cases in which tribal opinions are conflicting, exhibit developers should adhere to the most restrictive request.

The museum staff should also take care to involve individuals from various generations in their consultations. Older generations often distrust museums and institutional personnel more than younger generations and may take a firmer stand against assisting or working with non-Native entities. In their lifetimes, these elders often saw the most aggressive assimilation policies and faced the worst of the efforts designed to eradicate tribes. Because these experiences create different understandings and values, this can put museums and research institutions at odds with Native peoples. Inviting various age groups to participate in the consultation process can add challenges to the museum staff, but it will ultimately provide a fuller picture of the tribal perspective.

Two Specific Examples of Collaboration

The Heritage Center has recently participated in two collaborations with non-Native museums—one that was generally positive and one that was negative. In the past year we collaborated on a project with a local Oklahoma City museum to create an exhibit about the well-known Native American athlete and Olympian, Jim Thorpe, who was both Sac & Fox and Citizen Potawatomi. There was some reservation when we were first contacted because Thorpe's Sac & Fox heritage is often the only one acknowledged. We were pleased to learn that the Citizen Potawatomi were going to receive the same amount of space and attention as the Sac & Fox Nation. It demonstrated to us that the museum staff had conducted the proper research about Jim Thorpe and recognized that though Thorpe was enrolled as a member of the Sac & Fox Nation, he recognized both tribal affiliations. The museum exceeded our expectation in trying to tell a more complete story of Thorpe's life, and the exhibit was better because of it.

Unfortunately, not all of our partnerships have been so productive. For several years members of the Citizen Potawatomi Nation have worked to reach an agreement with the St. Mary's Historical Society in St. Mary's, Kansas, to transfer ownership of a census book for the Citizen Potawatomi from the 1860s. We have not been successful in arranging a transfer of ownership, but we have been able to come to an agreement that has eased some of the tribe's concerns about how the book is being presented and the conditions under which it is housed. Negotiations have been long and at time contentious, but we all work to keep the lines of communication open in hopes that in the coming years we will be able to resolve the matter and bring the census book to the Heritage Center, where it can be preserved in ideal conditions and be available to a larger audience.

Cultural objects that have found their way into museum collections often have deep cultural significance and sentimental value for tribes. Some tribes may feel like they are better stewards for that object than an outside museum or institute. In the case with the census book, those are the names and signatures of our ancestors, which were recorded at a vital time in Citizen Potawatomi history. It is much more than just a census book. As long as the objects are being cared for properly, and museum staffs are open, the relationship between the museum and the tribe can usually remain positive.

Our most successful collaborations have been with other tribes that have established, or are in the process of establishing, a cultural center of their own. In the first years after we opened our facility in 2006 we were invited out to consult with the Comanche Nation of Oklahoma, which had recently purchased a building that would become their cultural center and museum. We discussed the hurdles and pitfalls the Heritage Center experienced and were able to have an open dialogue about the challenges that we, as members of the tribe, face when deciding how to portray hundreds of years of complicated and fascinating history in a finite space and on a realistic budget. We also met with members of the Chickasaw Nation as they were planning the Chickasaw Nation Cultural Center and the Muscogee (Creek) Nation Museum, Cultural Center, and Archives sent three separate delegations to consult while they were working on their building.

Working with Removed Tribes in Their Ancestral Territories

The practice of Indian removal means that there are many tribes residing in territories that are geographically distant from their homelands. Museum staffs that are working with a tribe that was removed need to take the history of that tribe into consideration and understand the modern implications of removal. The museum should be aware that each tribe has a unique history, and their experiences will influence how and what they want emphasized in an exhibit about them.

The Citizen Potawatomi Nation is one of seven Potawatomi tribes recognized by the U.S. government. In addition, there are two Potawatomi Canadian First Nations. In many ways, we tell the same stories, and a visitor to the Citizen Potawatomi Nation Cultural Heritage Center in Oklahoma, the Forest County Potawatomi Cultural Center, Library, & Museum in Wisconsin, or the Hannahville Indian Community's Potawatomi Heritage Center in Michigan would notice that a majority of the objects and stories would be similar. We are all Woodlands people—*Neshnabek*—we speak the same language, and our ancestors followed common spiritual practices. The social and kinship bonds that form Native groups also facilitate wide-ranging professional networks. Despite geographic and historical diversity, we regularly collaborate with other Potawatomi communities to actively engage in academic research, exhibition and program development, and historic preservation. All of our cooperatives aid in strengthening and perpetuating Potawatomi bonds.

There are, however, areas of emphasis within the museum narratives that are different from one another. The removal era had a greater impact on the Citizen Potawatomi than most of the other Potawatomi tribes. Removals and loss of land dominate the narrative of our history for most of the nineteenth century. The history of the Citizen Potawatomi in our home territory ends with removal; however, museums in our ancestral territory need to continue our story into Kansas and Indian Territory because this is part of the whole story.

Conclusion

Many of the issues that may arise for museum staff working with Native Americans can be avoided by establishing a vision or goal for the project from the beginning. Present the goals and vision for the project to tribal members or their representatives with a clear scope of work that adheres to cultural and professional ethics. Museum staff must also be willing to work closely with the community to develop or alter the project plan and outcomes, if necessary, or even abandon an exhibit idea if tribal members protest. Museums will have greater success partnering with tribes if they start a project working with tribal consultants to create ideas and themes together and share ownership from the beginning.

Note

1. Pan-Indian is a term referring to music, symbols, dress, and customs sometimes adopted by displaced Indian people living in urban centers who have been detached from their specific cultural traditions. Non-Native people often identify these expressions as being part of all Native culture. Powwows and use of the "big drum" are two examples of pan-Indianism.

CHAPTER 4

Building Partnerships and Authority Sharing

> Today it is de rigueur for curators to involve [Native people]—as advisors, consultants, or co-curators—in museum representations of their culture. This is certainly an improvement over the situation in the past when a white, usually male, curator decided by himself the theme and content of an exhibition. It does not, however, solve the problems of the situation of Native people in the contemporary world.[1]

IN THE PREVIOUS chapter, the concept of authority sharing was introduced, which requires that everyone involved in a project be valued for the unique perspectives they bring, and all are given equal respect. For Native advisors this is especially important. Part of the legacy of colonialism is that Native people have had the authority to tell their own stories taken away. This has given rise, in part, to Native cultural centers and museums, places where Native people can share with their community and beyond, those things that they know to be true, without having to argue or justify them to others. Cultural centers and tribal museums will continue to play an expanding role in telling Native stories outside of the reservation, but not all tribes have a museum. For those communities, it is particulary important to be at the table, sharing tribal perspectives and histories.

Author Laura Peers evaluated the role and impact of Native people interpreting their historic communities at living history sites in her book *Playing Ourselves*, and she shares that "Native people have indicated a strong desire to participate in the creation and delivery of representations about their peoples, and there are important reasons that they should do so."[2]

Building Partnerships

When building a team for any project involving Native collections or history, identifying the right partners and knowing a little bit about them is an important first step. You may find that not all of the people identified can come together at the same time, for logistical reasons, but also because conflicting opinions or a history of disagreement would make such a gathering uncomfortable and unproductive for all involved. Often, archaeologists and Native cultural leaders disagree about the origins of a tribe or the relevance of oral history in understanding the past, among other things. It is unacceptable to ask a tribal elder or oral history keeper to attend a planning meeting where someone else on the team may challenge their knowledge (or already have challenged tribal knowledge in publications or lectures and alienated the tribe in the process). "Historically, mainstream museums have been considered the center of knowledge making; in this version Native American communities are represented on the periphery or frontier of discovery, the content but not the authors."[3] Respecting the rights of Native people to be authors of their own stories is vital to the success of *any* collaborative relationship.

Make sure to plan meetings on or near tribal communities.[4] This serves a couple of purposes; first, it allows Native people to share stories about their people, history, and culture in the communities in which the stories are vital. Team members can expect a greater depth of understanding and respect for the community, and advisors from the community may be more open and willing to share in their home territory, rather than in a museum. Being in tribal communities allows Native advisors to participate more in building the project and agenda. It also respects the fact that some advisors may not be comfortable in the museum setting and will be less likely to share if they feel uncomfortable. If there are advisors on the team who are not Native, being in a Native community will reinforce the importance of authority sharing. Finally, spending time in Native communities helps recognize Native people as modern and become more connected to values and concerns for the tribes today. These important insights will spill over into the project as it develops and will eventually impact visitors who come to see the final product.

When working with tribal advisors, make sure to understand their areas of expertise. Tribal advisors cannot speak on behalf of all Native people, or even represent all the various opinions within the tribal community of which he or she is a member. This may seem like common sense, but many Native advisors have said that they feel held to unrealistic expectations about the extent of their knowledge. Tribal historians will have extensive expertise about the history of the tribe, but may not necessarily be knowledgeable about traditional medicines, for example. Take the time to ask your advisors "who should be involved in this project," and ask them to help facilitate an introduction.

Be open to the various ways that tribal communities retain and pass on traditions and cultural knowledge. Tribal advisors may not speak their Native language or know how to create traditional arts; this, however, does not diminish their expertise in other areas. Brian Reynolds of the Maliseet shared, "There's pressure from film and media about what it means to be a 'real' Indian in today's world. People expect you to speak your language, drum or dance, make baskets, or fit other pop culture stereotypes. But I think now people carry forward what they can. Whether it be language, drumming, basket making, hunting or other activities. I don't think even in days gone by that *one* person was an expert at *all* activities. There were hunters, there were basket makers, etc. People pass on and carry forward what they can. There is no shame in that."[5]

In her review of the history of the Oneida Museum, Kristina Ackley points out that "Non-Natives have the power to hold Native Americans to unrealistic and damaging standards in determining what makes an 'authentic Indian.' But Indigenous people have not been passive victims without agency. They effectively help to shape the discourse of what is authentic and what is not, able to shape outsiders' perceptions of them even as they are often on the losing side of vastly unequal power relationships."[6]

When planning team meetings, expect healthy debate and discussions; however, be sensitive to the balance of power that people bring with them to the process. In some Native communities it is not acceptable to confront another person, and silence speaks louder than any words. Pay close attention to body language and silences, which may indicate that Native advisors are not feeling comfortable or respected. If debate starts to feel heated or disrespectful, make sure a strong facilitator is present, ready to bring people back on track. If authority sharing is not going well, the project will face new obstacles that can alienate team members and slow down progress. If there is a risk that disagreement will not be respectful or productive, schedule meetings comprised of smaller focus groups, and synthesize this information in-house after the fact.

When Disagreements Arise

Not all disagreement will come from Native and non-Native interactions. There can be disagreements within Native communities as well. Donald Soctomah, Passamaquoddy Tribal Historian, has said, "Native people are held to an unrealistic expectation that we all agree on everything. Just because one person is okay with the use of certain words or images doesn't mean that everyone agrees. You don't see this with other cultures. Everyone expects American[s] to disagree and it's okay, but if Native people disagree about something they're accused of factionalism."[7] Ackley shares the same perspective, saying, "it is unrealistic to assume that a diverse community will agree on everything. In this way, factionalism can be seen as continual, if episodic, rather than as a solely negative force."[8]

For some tribes, there is disagreement and debate about the kinds of objects and knowledge that are acceptable to share with others—even among tribal members. In some tribes, certain religious practices and ceremonies fall under the care of a limited number of people and are not to be shared outside of that group. For the Oneida community in Wisconsin, discussions about what kinds of information should be shared was an evolving debate in the development of an exhibit featuring religious objects. A group of tribal members said, " 'The non-Indian public does not have the right to examine, interpret, or present these beliefs, functions, and duties of the secret medicine societies of the Haudenosunee.' Those who protested the exhibit also did so in terms that challenged the standard anthropological view that every part of a culture is open to the public, in part to provide the opportunity for community dialogue on the issue."[9]

There are many questions that bubble up from the core concepts of intellectual ownership, considerations about collections, or stories that are based on societies, clans, or subgroups within the tribe; should they be exhibited at all? Who has the authority to say "yes, we can share that," and in the sharing out, does the interpretation need to be done by an insider, who has a more full understanding of the meaning? Ackley cites these discussions within the Oneida exhibit process as well, "some of those people who at first supported the exhibit came to cede authority to those who have more knowledge of such things, viewing it as a struggle they do not understand and therefore do not have the ability or the desire about which to make decisions."[10]

Disagreement within tribes can extend past differing opinions about access to cultural traditions and information or the use of certain objects. Tribes have survived hundreds of years of colonial oppression, and one legacy of this history is that individuals, families, and governments have made differing and difficult decisions about survival strategies. Historical and intergenerational trauma is real in Indian communities, yet can be ignored or disparaged by non-Native people. "Acculturation and tradition are not fixed positions that can be assigned to certain groups of people; rather they are a fluid force through which people navigate in their understanding of 'the what and the how' of being Oneida."[11]

Navigating factions within a tribe can be challenging. One thing to keep in mind and share with tribal advisors is that by asking to work with individual Native advisors, the museum staff are not taking sides but are seeking to represent the various perspectives and experiences in the community, as complex as that may be. Be transparent in the goals, and who is being consulted—both Native and non-Native advisors. Elected officials and tribal employees always need to be consulted; even if some members of the tribe contest their positions, they are the legal, elected, officials for the tribe. If there are one or more other groups who speak out against those officials, seek them out as well. This is another example when smaller focus groups will better serve the project goals than gathering Native advisors into one large meeting. This will require a longer project timeline, so make sure these considerations are taken into account during the planning and research phase.

Consider What the Museum Can Give Back

When working with tribal advisors, take the opportunity to think creatively with them about how this project and team can support community goals or strengthen community gaps. For example, in many tribes Native language loss is a deep concern. Elders are the primary speakers remaining in most communities, and the history of boarding schools, where students were brutally punished for speaking their language, has left generations of Native people unable to speak their language. The youngest generations are attending language programs in many reservation schools, but without the ability to speak it in the home, language retention is a challenge. Creating a community-wide gathering to share information and opinions about the subject of the project and ask for feedback, ideas, or to ask people to respond to a specific question could be a service for the community, bringing people together to share stories and language. One such example occurred during a "planning conference held in 1997, when men and women from the Alutiiq culture area gathered to talk about the old days and ways forward."[12] Language can also be incorporated into many aspects of exhibit or program development as a means of sharing unique or important cultural perspectives. It has also been used in administrative functions and training sessions for staff and board members to gain better insight into the values of the cultures represented by the museum.

One of the most common forms of Native/non-Native collaborations in museums is through exhibits. Certainly this is a good place to start building relationships. Because most museum visitors come to museums for exhibits, this creates one of the best opportunities to transform how Native people are represented in museums and American society. Ivan Karp says, "Exhibitions . . . are political arenas in which definitions of identity and culture are asserted and contested."[13] As mentioned previously, museum staffs seeking partnership or advice from Native advisors need to be flexible and ready to grow the project under the advice of Native consultants. Peers points out that "trying to fit Native histories and experiences into existing dominant society . . . is a patronizing level of inclusion that fails to grant real authority to Native peoples, and has resulted in the decision by some Native communities not to work with heritage agencies."[14]

Collaborating with Native advisors can create new opportunities to interpret objects and inspire interest in history. Patricia Erikson points out that "attempts to influence mainstream museums at the regional and national level are a critical part of (Native) strategies to survive as a distinct people. Along with textbooks, films, and other media, museums are targeted as important sites of representation that influence public perception of and actions toward Native peoples."[15]

Two Collaborative Exhibit Examples

At the Abbe Museum in Bar Harbor, Maine, two recent exhibits were transformed though the participation of Native advisors and curators. In the first example, the Abbe had purchased a collection consisting primarily of archival materials about a Penobscot woman named Lucy Nicolar who traveled the country performing under the stage name Princess Watahwaso in the early 1900s. Nicolar returned to Maine later in life and became a political, cultural, and artistic leader in her community. Had the show been created internally, it may have focused on the objects and the story of their acquisition. The Abbe had already identified the need to work with Native curators more frequently "to strengthen tribal relations to ensure a balanced Wabanaki perspective in content, planning, and museum governance."[16] The Tribal Historian for the Penobscot, James Eric Francis, Sr., was invited to serve as curator for the exhibit, which opened in October 2010. Lucy was known as "Aunt Lou" to everyone in the tribe, which became the exhibit title, expressing the deep personal relations she made that are important to tribal members to this day. The Tribal Historian was able to create an exhibit about Aunt Lou that shared with visitors who she was and why she was an important leader for the community. It even included a genealogy chart that linked modern tribal family members to her causes, as a visual representation of how impactful one person can be. The chart identified descendants who are basket makers—important to her work revitalizing basket traditions—or political leaders—important to her efforts to bring the right to vote in state elections to the tribe in the 1960s. Not only did this perspective create a personal, engaging exhibit that visitors enjoyed, but it also created new learning for the Penobscot Nation about this important ancestor. *Aunt Lou* was successful because of the personal tone the exhibit had, which was a result of hiring a Native curator. When the exhibit concluded at the Abbe, it traveled to the Penobscot tribe and was exhibited at the school.

Working with Native curators and advisors can lead to exhibits about topics that are challenging for museum visitors and staff. Native advisors can help identify topics for exhibits about contemporary issues, sovereignty, colonialism, and regional history that may be overlooked in museums, schools, and community commemorations. Native advisors need the freedom to incorporate these difficult topics because it is a more accurate representation of their history, culture, and modern life. Museum exhibits and interpretation are often criticized for including Native history only when interpreting the past. A common exhibit formula is to present history as a timeline, starting with Native peoples from the region, then European or American settlers move in, and the Indian story disappears as the interpretation continues with history focused on white and immigrant stories. This form of narrative was so common that "in 1977 the Mohawk of Kahnawake decided to establish a cultural center instead of a museum because they perceived the museum's exclusive focus on the past to be antithetical to their mandate of fostering future cultural development and the revitalization of tradition."[17]

The second exhibit at the Abbe Museum, *Headline News: Wabanaki Sovereignty in the 21st Century*, changed the way the museum understood its responsibilities and relationships with the tribes in Maine. Abbe staff was concerned by public comments shared online at regional newspaper websites about the four federally recognized tribes in Maine, collectively known as the Wabanaki. The comments represented deeply held stereotypes and bias about Native people and did not serve to create an inclusive community. In 2010, the Curator of Education worked with the four federally recognized tribes to identify eight topics commonly misunderstood about modern Wabanaki sovereignty. The Abbe exhibit team researched newspaper coverage of the topics and selected headlines to use in each section as a means of introducing visitors to the way the topics are covered in the media. The team then spent hours with each community interviewing elders, political and cultural leaders, historians, and natural resource directors. The comments from these interviews made up the bulk of the exhibit. Everything addressed in the exhibit spoke to projects the tribes were working on as an extension of their sovereignty; partnerships and collaborations with private organizations or communities that they wanted the public to be aware of; and ways in which they were maintaining their cultural and political sovereignty.

There were some community members who felt the topic was too contentious and expressed concern about the exhibit, but overwhelmingly, the tribes were enthusiastic to participate and have the opportunity to share more about their modern life. For those who were concerned, Abbe staff listened to the concerns and worked to address them in the structure of the exhibit. Some interviews were conducted as listening sessions, with the goal of leaving all involved feeling heard and respected for their points of view. Other tribal members chose not to participate in interviews at all, but an offer to talk was extended to everyone interested. Abbe staff did not interview non-Native people for this exhibit, unless they were an official representative for the tribe. This occurred most often within the natural resource departments, where not all employees were Native. Authority sharing occurred between tribal nations and within the tribes themselves. It was understood that non-Native perspective about the topics, and sovereignty itself, was sufficiently shared and represented in the exhibit through the newspaper headlines and therefore was not necessary in interviews.

Visitor comments from Native and non-Native people alike proved there was an interest in the topic and people learned much about modern Indian life. Not everyone who attended agreed, however, and the Abbe received comments with statements like "Too political, no culture," and "not enough objects, too much about politics, no real culture."[18] These comments served as evidence of the importance of focusing on contemporary issues in exhibits, because modern life *is* what makes Native culture alive and distinct. Visitor expectations that Indian objects have to be old or fit American notions of "traditional" in terms of materials and techniques reinforce stereotypes of Native people living in the past. By breaking through these stereotypes, the exhibit challenged assumptions about what it means to be Native American today.

As a result of more inclusive collaborative relationships, there are examples of new techniques for exhibiting and interpreting Native stories. Native advisors will often focus more on storytelling than objects. Museums are known for their collections; it is what makes a museum unique, and so it can be hard to think about stories first, then objects. But this is often what tribal museums and cultural centers do, and they do it very well. "I would argue that it is necessary for exhibit developers, if they hope to convey the continuance of Native cultural traditions, to abandon the idea of allowing objects to lead content (especially since a majority of the objects in museum collections are historic pieces) and instead allow for concepts to drive decisions about exhibit content."[19] Exhibits at the National Museum of the American Indian, and many other museums small and large around the country, are structured around topics and themes, rather than chronologically or objects based.

Telling stories in a nonlineal framework can jar visitors from their expectations and signal to them that they are about to learn something in a new way. At the National Museum of the American Indian, the exhibit *All Roads Are Good* "paired contemporary and historic objects to foreground cultural survival and historical continuations of cultural processes, despite change."[20]

James Clifford reviewed once such exhibit in Alaska, crediting the museum with helping to "turn around local prejudices about being Native" and commented that, "While the presentation was strongly historical, enlarged color pictures of individuals (drying salmon, picking berries), video recordings, and images of contemporary villages reminded viewers of the present moment—of whose heritage this was. The exhibit themes—'Our Ancestors,' 'Our History,' 'Our Way of Living,' 'Our Beliefs,' and 'Our Family'—sustained a focus on community. The old objects, returning after a century and still linked with specific places and people, provoked emotional reactions—sadness, recognition, gratitude, kinship. . . . Cultural continuity through change was manifested by juxtaposing ancient, historical, and contemporary objects and images."[21]

Conclusion

Museums have the power to transform the lives of staff and stakeholders, and the lives of our visitors. Inclusive collaborations with tribal partners acknowledge their authority to determine what stories they want to tell and how they want them told. Amy Lonetree, professor of American studies at the University of California–Santa Cruz, sums up this potential as follows:

As we look to the future, I believe it is critical that museums support Indigenous communities in our efforts toward decolonization, through privileging Indigenous voice and perspective, through challenging stereotypical representations of Native people that were produced in the past, and by serving as educational forums for our own communities and the general public. Furthermore, the hard truths of our history need to be conveyed, both for the good of our communities and the general public, to a nation that has willfully sought to silence our versions of the past.[22]

CASE STUDY: *NATIVE VOICES*

A PERMANENT GALLERY AT THE NATURAL HISTORY MUSEUM OF UTAH

Becky Menlove, Associate Director for Visitor Experience

In one of ten permanent exhibits at the Natural History Museum of Utah, *Native Voices* introduces visitors to the indigenous people of Utah and the surrounding region—Ute, Shoshone, Goshute, Paiute, and Navajo—and their distinctive geographies, histories, languages, and material culture. Continuity and change within Native communities is interpreted through first-person narratives, juxtaposition of contemporary and historic objects and images, original film and audio programs, a language interactive, and public programming. The exhibit provides insights into vibrant cultural groups whose distinct histories, traditions, tragedies, and triumphs inform the present and future in both tribal and mainstream life.

The Natural History Museum of Utah has no permanent Native American staff, nor does it employ an ethnographic curator or scholar, so it is absolutely essential that we consult and collaborate with Native people on an ongoing basis. Finding the right approach and level of engagement for each project, however, is best done on a case-by-case basis.

Native Voices was developed in consultation and collaboration with a large contingent of Native people with the intent to provide a forum for expanding awareness and appreciation of the continuum of Utah's American Indians. The exhibition aims to encourage reflection on personal perceptions of American Indians and their histories and to question how those perceptions may have been formed and become generalized over time; to promote understanding and appreciation of Utah-specific American Indian cultures; and to provide insights about Indian perspectives of critical historical moments and how those moments play out in contemporary times.

A Complex Context: Envisioning a New Natural History Museum

In 2011, the Natural History Museum of Utah (NHMU) opened a new state-of-the-art facility in the foothills of Salt Lake City. The site, the building, and ten permanent exhibitions were designed to embody the museum's mission: to illuminate the natural world and the place of humans within it (Figure 4.1).

Through many years of feasibility studies, conceptual plans, fundraising, and negotiating, the idea was headed toward reality by 2000 when I arrived at the museum. Senior staff and curators were developing a vision for the museum and writing the new mission, which continues to guide our work.

In those early conversations, a global approach to the human experience was envisioned. Curatorial staff imagined a fluid and integrated journey through time and space underpinned by the interconnected web of life. From fossil evidence of the deep past to archaeological and ethnographic collections reflecting more recent change, the galleries

Figure 4.1. Land Terrace at the Natural History Museum of Utah. Photo by Stuart Ruckman, Copyright NHMU

would tell complex stories of the natural world and reveal the interconnection of all life forms, including humans, linked through evolution and the flow of energy. A culminating gallery experience, *Utah Futures*, would invite visitors to engage in reflection about how natural systems work and what it means for them now and into the future. Although this approach provided a powerful framework for most of the museum's permanent galleries—indeed this is very much the experience our visitors encounter through most of these spaces—it presented serious problems in terms of interpreting indigenous collections and cultures.

It was a plan that did not take into account the difficult and often contentious relationships American Indians have long endured with regard to museums and universities in which objects have been collected, studied, and displayed without regard to the people who can best interpret these materials. It also suggested the juxtaposition of dinosaurs and other extinct animals with the material culture of ancient people and past generations of extant Native people. This approach, as in natural history museum collections and exhibits of the past, strongly suggests a story of vanishing and not one of continuity and lively contemporary cultures that our ethnographic collections document.

And because our archaeological and ethnographic collections do not tell the entire human story, we would soon have found ourselves setting apart Native people as unique in this integration with natural systems. It quickly became clear that the cultural stories we have to tell at NHMU are those connected with our collections, and those stories deserve their own space and the open discussion of the people whom they represent. Paul Chaat

Smith has written, "At different times the narrative of this country has said we [Indians] didn't exist and the land was empty; then it was mostly empty and populated by fearsome savages; then populated by noble savages who couldn't get with the program; and on and on. Today the equation is Indian equals spiritualism and environmentalism. In twenty years it will probably be something else."[23] Despite the potential to have overlain environmentalism or other external narratives on Indian history and culture, we opted instead to create a separate gallery—a cultural pavilion of sorts—for *Native Voices*.

A Firm Foundation: NHMU Indian Advisory Committee

For decades, the museum has relied on an Indian Advisory Committee (IAC) to confer on all matters relating to American Indian collections and programs. Established well in advance of such advisory groups born of the Native American Graves Protection and Repatriation Act (NAGPRA) regulations, the IAC has been consulted about collections, interpretation, incoming and in-house exhibit plans, programs and partnerships, and of course, some repatriation issues (although a separate committee now oversees this). Former Museum Director Donald Hague established the committee in the 1980s and Ann Hanniball, now Associate Director for Community Relations, has presided over this group since 1992. No term limits are employed regarding service on this committee, and several members have held their positions since the beginning.

NHMU relies on the committee to advise us directly and also to provide guidance about whom to consult from within their communities. The IAC includes representatives from each of Utah's federally recognized tribes; the Director of the State Office of Indian Affairs; University of Utah faculty and staff associated with Indian education and support services; a University of Utah Indian Student Association member; a representative from the Urban Indian Center of Salt Lake City; and community members at large. Community representatives are invited to serve based on their expertise and positions in various organizations, whereas tribal representatives are sought through appointment by tribal leadership.

This approach has been appreciated by tribal leaders and is appropriate in dealing with sovereign nations; certainly a similar approach is taken when looking for advisors from other governmental bodies. Many years ago, the Northwestern Band of Shoshone appointed Patty Timbimboo Madsen to serve on the IAC as part of her job as Cultural/Natural Resources Manager. Because her job is not a political appointment, she has been able to continue on the IAC through many election cycles and many changes in leadership in her community. Appointments are not always so successful, however. Many of the tribes make political appointments for IAC membership. Because each tribe has its own election cycle and it is possible for the entire leadership of a tribe to turn over at the same time, it can be challenging to work on a long-term projects or recurring programs. You can find yourself without representation or inadvertently consulting with the wrong person in the midst of things.

This scenario occurred near the end of our *Native Voices* project. We had been working directly with Paiute Indian Tribe of Utah (PITU) Tribal Chair, Lora Tom, who had long been assigned to serve on the Museum's IAC. In 2011, when I sent a film crew to Cedar City to work on media elements for a *Native Voices* piece, I contacted Tom and she helped make arrangements with the crew. As shooting was about to begin, I heard from the crew and from the newly elected Tribal Chair Jeannine Borchardt that I had overstepped protocol by not checking in with her. Apparently, after serving multiple terms, Tom had been replaced as chair, and although I assumed she was still serving as IAC representative, I was clearly wrong. Borchardt quickly stepped into this position in time for final work on the project and for the opening of the museum. She served in this capacity during her two-year term. A new Paiute Indian Tribe of Utah Tribal Chairwoman, Gari Lafferty, has just been elected and will now serve on the IAC.

Sometimes, when a committee member resigns, as did Roland McCook of the Northern Ute tribe back in 2001, it can be difficult to get a new designee assigned. When McCook left we were unable to find a replacement. Current tribal leadership was silent on the matter. We were in the middle of creating an exhibition about Utah's tribes for the 2002 Cultural Olympiad, and the tribes were also occupied with preparations to participate in the opening ceremonies. We reached out to Forrest Cuch (Northern Ute), then Director of the State Office of Indian Affairs, who was representing broader Indian concerns on the IAC and also to filmmaker Larry Cesspooch (Northern Ute). Together they agreed to serve as representatives of the Northern Ute tribe for the remainder of the project, so we continued on without a tribally appointed person.

In a conversation with McCook many years later, he suggested a different approach to finding consultants and garnering permission to work on tribal lands with tribal members. In regard to working with the Northern Ute tribe, whose elections are often contentious, and whose business council is often overwhelmed, he recommended that I contact tribal offices—nonpolitical staff members—and simply tell them our plans rather than waiting for broad business council approval in advance. This approach has been successful in a number of ways.

Cesspooch, who stepped in during the making of our Cultural Olympiad exhibition, has continued to collaborate with the museum on many projects and remains a good friend and a reliable consultant. He collaborated with me throughout the development of *Native Voices*, joining meetings, providing stories and images, sharing his and his community's history, guiding me to other resources, and reviewing plans and materials as they were prepared. I asked how he felt about being an ad-hoc representative of the Northern Ute tribe in the midst of political upheaval in the community. We had spoken before about the difficulty of truly representing an entire community rather than simply sharing one's own experience within that community. At the time of our meeting, he was among those "on the outs" with newly elected and contested tribal leadership, and he made it clear that he was not speaking on behalf of the tribe but rather as a Ute person, which was a perspective he was fully authorized to share. Of course even when assigned and sanctioned by a tribe's leaders, it is clear that an individual can rarely fully speak for an entire community.

Cesspooch spoke to me recently about collaborating. He said, "I always try to help people understand; it's the only way to get respect. I look at it as a great honor to be able to leave something that would show what's been presented in the past, what it's like to be Ute and to live this way. It's still here, alive and well. So, to see the drawings and all the conceptual stuff; I really felt privileged to see it come to fruition. I was just privileged to be involved and to see it gel and to see it grow. That's what it's all about. That's a good ride."[24]

Although Cesspooch is still not assigned by the tribe to serve on the IAC, Hanniball continues to invite his participation, and I always enjoy calling on his expertise. In a conversation with Donna Land (Northern Ute), an IAC member-at-large, she noted that whether tribal leadership appoints an individual, it is essential that the tribes have representation on the committee. She acknowledged her gratitude that Cesspooch continues to participate.

I learned early on that interpretive programs developed for the general public can be low priority for small tribes whose resources are stretched thin and whose work focuses for the most part on such issues as economic development, natural resource management, education, housing, and the health and human services desperately needed in their communities. At my first tribal leaders' meeting at which Ann Hanniball and I were introducing an exhibition project, other items on the agenda included raging wildfires on reservation lands, contentious water rights litigation, a battle for the sovereign right to bring nuclear waste to tribal land, and a crisis of increased incidence of cancer among members of the Ute tribe. Against this backdrop, a cultural program aimed at outside audiences held little sway in terms of its urgency. And yet, based on participation among tribal communities over time, it appears there are good reasons for tribes to collaborate on this level and for museums to provide a venue in which Indian history can be told from an Indian perspective.

NHMU has been fortunate in its ongoing relationship with dedicated IAC members and their willingness to share their culture, tell their stories, and educate the community at large about the people whose homelands we occupy.

Ceceilia Tso (Navajo), an IAC member from the university community, suggests a need for the type of interpretation we were aiming for: "As a kid, you look at things as normal. And then you become older, and you wonder why things have happened to you or what's the reasoning behind some of the dysfunction in the family—alcoholism and drugs and diabetes and health care and people being sick and dying around you at a very rapid rate. I didn't really understand what all of that meant. What is abuse? What is historical trauma? What is the history? We don't really learn American Indian history, our cultural history. [In mainstream education] you get a very distorted view of what American history is."[25]

We know from surveys and visitor studies that NHMU audiences are interested in learning about Utah's Native people with particular emphasis on historic objects and their manufacture, resources used by indigenous people historically, what tribes live in the area, what kinds of dwellings Utah's Indians built in the past, and what languages are spoken by the Indians in the region.[26] It is also clear, based on the experiences of our collaborators, that there is much about Native life in Utah that Utahns do not know. Genevieve Fields of the Confederated Tribes of Goshute has said "there are lots of misconceptions about Native people: that all Indians are poor, they live in tipis, they take government handouts, they eat different food and live in a different way from mainstream communities." She suggests that the museum could be an important conduit for the truth about Indian communities—"to clarify what's real; to make real connections."[27] Gwen Cantsee recognizes the same issues:

> Salt Lake City is integrated pretty much now with all the different cultures. But there is always a little bit of—I don't know how to say this—people look at you, 'hey, there's an Indian.' I even ran into this one young kid, he was ten or eleven years old, one time when I was in Salt Lake, and he kept looking at me while we were walking around in Target. He

> kept looking at me and he finally came over to me and he asked me, do you live in a tipi? I said, no—but sometimes in the summertime. And he just looked at me. And it's kind of surprising to know that in this day and age, the young kids still have the perception, that, yeah, we ride around on horses everywhere, live in tipis, go out and hunt buffalo.[28]

These experiences and others seem to have led to changes in the way Indian communities may be thinking about the usefulness of collaborating with museums. In my early work with Native consultants, projects typically focused on one-way sharing. The museum would aim to create an authentic and honest interpretation of objects from which interested visitors would learn and appreciate Indian culture and art. Native consultants would willingly provide information, correct misconceptions and stereotypes, and provide other insights. However, the same consultants and their communities rarely considered the finished exhibit or program to be something for them.

During the years of preparation for *Native Voices* I witnessed a paradigm shift among communities with whom I was working. It seemed that a willingness to collaborate was something different from simply consulting. Working together could result in a meaningful place for Native people as well as for non-Native visitors. Cantsee, White Mesa Ute Chairwoman, suggested that the new museum "should present pertinent issues, stories, exhibits that you'd feel comfortable taking your kids to. It should be a place to teach some of the cultural traditions and values that have slipped away. A place to say 'here's a story I didn't tell you, but you need to know.'"[29]

Similarly, Stephanie Holly, Navajo representative for IAC, recommended that *Native Voices* should make Navajos comfortable and provide an important service to tribal members who visit. "The exhibit should tell the Navajo stories—what they believe and where they came from, where they've been, and where they are today. And celebrate the Navajo language. While young and urban Navajos sometimes don't know the language, it is significant and important. It can help them to understand where they're from and to communicate with elders. The stories aren't the same in English. They lose their meaning."[30]

The Creation of Native Voices

To energize and fully engage the IAC in the development of the new building and exhibits, as the design phase for *Native Voices* was about to begin, Hanniball invited tribal leaders to review their appointees and to approve their participation in the development of this big project. Both the Navajo Nation and Confederated Tribes of Goshute assigned new designees. NHMU then arranged for the IAC to travel together with the design team to the National Museum of the American Indian in Washington, D.C., and to its collections facility in Suitland, Maryland.

The group was at once thrilled at the significance of the building and its exhibits and dismayed to see that Utah tribes were virtually absent from the interpretive program. For nearly twenty years, the museum's advisory group had recommended that NHMU focus on the indigenous people of Utah in our programs and exhibits, despite a much broader Indian demographic in Utah's cities, towns, and reservations. The lack of information about

Utah's tribes in the nation's Indian museum catalyzed this thinking; however, the committee agreed that although *Native Voices* would focus on the indigenous people of Utah, it would also acknowledge American Indians of other regions for whom Utah is now a home. In fact, changes in community makeup, tribal roles, mobility of families and individuals, and for some tribes, their thinking about blood quantum versus line-of-descent led to a more balanced inclusion of other indigenous groups in the exhibit content, which explores the push and pull of reservation versus urban life.

The collections facility at Suitland provided access to objects of Utah Indian origin, from baskets to cradles, as well as specialized spaces built to enhance Native participation in and ownership of the national museum and the collections it cares for. This lifted the spirits of our team and ignited conversation about the possibilities for NHMU. We returned with new insights and enthusiasm for the project in time for next steps.

The museum sits on historic Ute land, and the IAC was clear in its directives, tribe by tribe, about how *Native Voices* should look, the form it should take, and feelings it should convey. Cantsee said, "It should feel welcoming and homey . . . and to have relevance, the exhibit must have a strong connection to the outdoors." Crissandra Murphy of the Confederated Tribes of Goshute at Ibapah said simply, "it should have photographs of the land here, which is home."[31] Patty Timbimboo Madsen of the Northwest Band of Shoshone shared, along with others, a desire that the exhibit sit directly on the ground, face the east, and be circular in form "to honor this meaningful symbol of life."[32]

Conversations with the IAC during master planning led to agreement that a gallery about the Native people of Utah and the surrounding region needed to be implicitly about the people; their place in the contemporary world, and their deep history in this region. Separate from the terracing interconnected exhibits elsewhere it would be designed to rest on the highest and easternmost edge of the building. This requirement presented many challenges for the design architects, but they rose to them all. *Native Voices* in its built form is a circle with a wide entry hall accessed from the *Sky* gallery. The space celebrates traditional homes of the indigenous people of this region (tipi, wikiup, and hogan) and honors the sacred circular form, not just in its exterior wall, but also with exhibit components moving inward in concentric rings (Figure 4.2). Visitors are invited to move through the space in a clockwise direction as one would move inside a traditional Native home. As hoped for, the gallery sits directly on the earth (it is slab on grade) so that no spaces or activities occur beneath it. The floor's surface is aggregate concrete (as close as we could come to an earthen floor). Walls and seating are made of naturally colored maple; the exterior wall made of interwoven maple slats references the importance of basket making among many of the tribes. A door at the eastern edge of the space invites visitors outside to an amphitheater formed of red sandstone where programs can be presented and where tribal communities can engage in activities if they choose.

Although there was a good deal of cross-cultural conversation and collaboration to get to this level of consensus on the architecture of the space, the design and interpretation within was a much more complicated and messy process. An enormous number of individuals participated over the course of the project, which had multiple stops and starts along the way.

To develop content and design for multiple galleries, I chose to assemble advisory teams, with one team for each gallery. This would allow us to augment the knowledge base within

Figure 4.2. Homeland mural by Kenneth Blackbird and maple walls with first-person stories. Photo by Stuart Ruckman, Copyright NHMU

our small curatorial staff, to bring broad interdisciplinarity into the discussion, and to open the conversations to blue-sky thinking. These large and diverse groups were gathered in the fall of 2005.

Decision-making authority was of course a key concern, and commitment and continuity among the consultants and collaborators was essential. We created a hierarchy for this process among the other exhibit teams, and although I served as the point person for *Native Voices*, the level and nature of the input we sought from the team was quite different from the other exhibit working groups. In addition to providing content ideas, comments, and recommendations, they were asked to participate in decision making in a number of areas and to share their personal and community stories. In the same way that the IAC helped to direct the architectural experience of the *Native Voices* gallery, they also drove our decisions to present a chronology of federal Indian policy through the experiences of Utah Indians, to present content through first-person narratives, to seek a Native photographer to gather images for the exhibition, and to provide a focus on language within the gallery content.

Lora Tom, an IAC representative, saw important opportunities in this type of collaboration and noted:

> Just to be part of the museum is an honor—a time for the tribe itself to be showcased. A time that individual stories can be told, whether it's small pictures that can be showed and shared, and a bit of history can be highlighted, a small tribe in southern Utah. Most tribes don't have the opportunity to do that. Look at the tribes here in Utah, those who have the resources, those who have much to survive on. And you also look at the tribes who maintain what they do have and who are grateful. But you look at the larger museums [in reference to National Museum of the American Indian] that have all these different types of photos and all sorts of things to glamorize themselves with, and then look at our smaller tribes who don't have that. So this is an opportunity, an opportunity that is not only going to impact the tribe itself but also the people in the state of Utah. I think that's a good thing. We want to show the people in the state of Utah that we are good people.

> We have the same type of plan—to live, survive, to love, to do well. We have no hidden agendas. We are just like anyone else. We just may be a different color. That's what I would like them to know about the tribe.[33]

At the table for *Native Voices* planning were the entire IAC; several NHMU staff; university anthropology, education, and Indian studies faculty; and independent scholars. Ralph Appelbaum Associates (RAA), an exhibit design firm, introduced their "integrated design process" and shared a broad theme statement they had developed: "Many indigenous peoples have inhabited North America for thousands of years; their accounts of their past and their present can instruct and enlighten us." With the intent of sparking discussion, the design team had generated many ideas to review with the working group, including potential topics: ethnography, American Indian experience in Utah, creation stories, tribes and the larger community, Utah-focused themes, Native literature and arts, and much more.

The museum's overarching themes of interconnection were also reintroduced at this meeting, with the suggestion that in *Native Voices*, it would be possible to examine such topics as evolution through work at the University of Utah focused on genetic connections among contemporaneous tribes and prehistoric people in Utah and elsewhere. This concept was not well received, and in a follow-up conversation with Dennis O'Roarke, whose work was referenced, he suggested that this topic did not seem appropriate for the sort of cultural content desired by the IAC. He chose to step down as an advisory group participant. Energy flow, diversity, and ecology were similarly rejected as not pertinent in the context of interpreting indigenous experience. Shirley Silversmith (Navajo/Apache) noted that despite romantic notions, she considers indigenous people to be highly attuned to nature and more aware of the damage that contemporary humans are inflicting on the land than the dominant culture. However, she did not see good reasons to separate nature into categories of ecology, diversity, and energy, nor to focus on these themes in this gallery.

Former member Cuch took the lead in directing the conversation toward pressing issues for Indian communities across the state. He eloquently spoke of what he called "generational memory" and the need for healing across multiple generations, which is a phenomenon in which the traumas of past generations continue to impact each new generation in myriad ways. He recommended that in *Native Voices* the history of Utah's Indians must be presented—the hard truths, the stories as experienced by Native people. He recommended that many voices be heard; that scholars and Native leaders participate in the development of content. And he suggested that the arc of Native experience in this region be illuminated.

Cuch's ideas laid the groundwork for the introductory sequence inside the gallery, but much more work was needed and many more voices had yet to be heard. I recommended that along with large-group meetings at the museum, I would begin to meet with committee members and their communities in their own territory. RAA prepared a lengthy questionnaire to guide this initial information quest, and over the course of the project, many trips were made around the state to work with tribal communities.

Through many touch points, exhibit content and components continued to collect, but not to coalesce.

Kathy Kankainen, NHMU collections manager for anthropology, assembled an object checklist, and then stepped in to create a cohesive content outline from which first-person narratives and exhibition text would be developed. Stephen Trimble, a Utah writer, was contracted to conduct research and interviews with tribal communities and to write introductory text for each major exhibit section. The goal was to create a layered approach to exhibit text that would include a literary/humanities voice for introductions, first-person narratives to elucidate primary storylines, and curatorial voice for object identification.

As the project progressed, the makeup of the *Native Voices* exhibit working group expanded and contracted, and many individuals contributed in deep and personal ways. Cesspooch shared an image and story of his son Sage's blessing with the eagle feather, an important spiritual ceremony, noting that "power is in the blood. Bishop Arrowchis, [giving the blessing] was my mother's uncle. The spiritual power came to me through my mother. It comes through the generations, and there is always someone that's willing to take up the work. . . . I feel privileged for the gifts I have. It takes me wherever I go. I don't panic; I just accept it."[34] Others invoked their family histories, tragedies, and triumphs in personal narratives and shared family photos, as well as agreeing to be photographed (Figure 4.3).

With the success of a National Endowment for the Humanities Implementation Grant in 2009, we were able to bring in a team of humanities scholars to confer with our IAC. Anthropologist Patricia Albers, Historian Ned Blackhawk, and Navajo scholar Harry Walters joined us for on-site meetings over the last two years of exhibit development and implementation and brought diverse perspectives, deep knowledge, new eyes, and helpful criticism to the project. Although the *Native Voices* advisory team had agreed that first-person narratives—the Native Voice—would be the authoritative voice in the exhibition, Albers and Blackhawk recommended that we add contextualizing introductions—dates, places, circumstances in the third person. In this way, visitors unfamiliar with events such as the Long Walk or the Bear River Massacre would better understand the meaning of the personal stories of these events. They reviewed and fact checked; they provided editorial comments on the sequencing and voice of curatorial text. They recommended editing of what they considered to be the somewhat "romanticized and new-agey" tone of the introductory text, and helped to

Figure 4.3. Object showcases and central storytelling area within Native Voices Gallery. Photo by Stuart Ruckman, Copyright NHMU

vet the enormous range of quotations gathered by Trimble, to help identify those most useful in providing an inclusive narrative. Not surprisingly, recommendations from the three scholars were not always in sync with each other or with those of the IAC. Revising the text to accommodate this wide-ranging input required balance, fairness—and of course, adherence to established word counts and accessibility standards for our audience.

Not every recommendation from the scholars was implemented. For example, section titles, as well as focus areas were drafted in the first person (e.g., "We Remember," "We've always been here," "We live in two worlds," "We are sovereign nations," and such). Albers felt that these were disingenuous if not attributed to individual speakers, but Indian advisors requested that these titles remain, and indeed, although there are no attributions for them, each phrase was spoken multiple times by many people during consultation.

Soon after the first scholar script review, and as I began to search for more urban-based images, I met Karyn Denny, a young photographer and Navajo from Monument Valley. My intent was to hire Denny for some additional photography, but our conversation led to much more input. Denny's opinion of the exhibition text was that it was old-fashioned and backward looking; that many quotes from community leaders of an older generation reflected ways of thinking and views of history that weren't pertinent to her generation. These insights helped to guide the work still remaining for the final section of the exhibition, formerly called "We're still here." It was at Denny's urging that we changed the title of this section to "New Choices, New Dreams." I began to reach out to other Native youth in the development of this final exhibit section. Likewise, as the production of the media, including a five-screen video for the exhibit was getting underway, the National Endowment for the Humanities advisors and the IAC agreed strongly that the treatment for this program would focus on youth.

As pre-production on the video proceeded, and Director Kate Raizs interviewed a wide variety of young people both in the city and on reservations, she began to find connections among the stories she was told: that elders and mentors were central to the stories.

The five-screen video—now an MUSE gold award winner—continues to inspire and engage visitors despite its fifteen-minute length. But it appears we still have work to do with regard to the youth population. In a meeting of the IAC in May 2013, which now includes new members, a tour of *Native Voices* elicited new perspectives on the gallery. I was not able to attend this meeting, but I am told that the objects and stories in the Utah tribes section focus only on "cradle boards and the accouterments of adulthood, but miss what comes between."

As is the case for all of the exhibit galleries, programs, and experiences at NHMU, we are evaluating *Native Voices*. We are learning about how visitors engage with the space, with the stories, and with the objects, and we are planning for remediation that may enhance or improve the experience. Our work will continue with the IAC as we make adjustments or changes and begin to expand the story to include more focus on Indian youth. During the development of this gallery, we often heard from community members that various projects bring people to Indian communities, they ask questions, they do their projects, and they never return. It's our goal to return, to maintain these relationships and to continue to make *Native Voices* relevant for the communities it celebrates.

Finding My Way into This Work

Although I am one of those non-Natives who does not always understand the root of things, I have deep respect for other people and I've learned to listen. And perhaps the central tenet of my success working with Indian communities for so many years is the acknowledgment that I am an outsider looking in. I always begin these cross-cultural projects with an open mind and the understanding that I have a lot to learn—and that not everything is meant to be shared. I think I have gained the trust of my collaborators because they know I will not misuse the information they generously give and I will not press for information that is not meant to be disclosed.

Notes

1. James Clifford, "Looking Several Ways: Anthropology and Native Heritage in Alaska," *Current Anthropology* 45, no. 1 (February 2004): 22.
2. Laura Peers, *Playing Ourselves Interpreting Native Histories at Historic Reconstructions* (Lanham, MD: Alta Mira Press, 2007), 66.
3. Patricia Pierce Erikson, "Decolonizing the 'Nation's Attic,'" in *The National Museum of the American Indian Critical Conversations*, edited by Amy Lonetree and Amana J. Cobb (Lincoln: University of Nebraska Press, 2008), 47.
4. Be prepared to reimburse tribal members for the cost of any travel they may incur to attend meetings or visit the museum.
5. Brian Reynolds., "Headline News: Wabanaki Sovereignty in the 21st Century," Abbe Museum exhibit online at http://www.abbemuseum.org/headline-news/Identity/HeadlineNewsIdentity.html.
6. Kristina Ackley, "Tsiʔniyukwalihoʔta, the Oneida Nation Museum Creating a Space for Haudenosaunee Kinship and Identity," in *Contesting Knowledge: Museums and Indigenous Perspectives*, edited by Susan Sleeper-Smith (Lincoln: University of Nebraska Press, 2009), 273.
7. Donald Sotomah, personal correspondence, October 2013.
8. Ackley, "Tsiʔniyukwalihoʔta," 273.
9. Ackley, "Tsiʔniyukwalihoʔta," 270.
10. Ackley, "Tsiʔniyukwalihoʔta," 273.
11. Ackley, "Tsiʔniyukwalihoʔta," 273.
12. Clifford, "Looking Several Ways," 11.
13. Peers, *Playing Ourselves*, 109.
14. Peers, *Playing Ourselves*, 48.
15. Erikson, "Decolonizing the 'Nation's Attic,'" 78.
16. Abbe Museum Strategic Plan, 2010–2014, http://www.abbemuseum.org/downloads/AbbeMuseumStrategicPlan2010-2014.pdf, p. 8.
17. Ruth B. Phillips, "Why Not Tourist Art? Significant Silences in Native American Museum Representations," in *After Colonialism: Imperial Histories and Postcolonial Displacements*, edited by Gyan Prakash (Princeton, NJ: Princeton University Press, 1994), 116.
18. Abbe visitor comment cards, 2010.

19. Amy Lonetree, *Decolonizing Museums: Representing Native America in National and Tribal Museums* (Chapel Hill: University of North Carolina Press, 2012), 47.
20. Erikson, "Decolonizing the 'Nation's Attic,'" 74.
21. Clifford, "Looking Several Ways," 22.
22. Amy Lonetree, "Museums as Sites of Decolonization: Truth Telling in National and Tribal Museums, " in *Contesting Knowledge: Museums and Indigenous Perspectives*, edited by Susan Sleeper-Smith (Lincoln: University of Nebraska Press, 2009), 334.
23. Paul Chaat Smith, *Everything You Know about Indians Is Wrong* (Minneapolis: University of Minnesota Press, 2009), 20.
24. Cesspooch, personal interview, 2013.
25. Tso, personal interview, 2008.
26. Visitor surveys conducted by K. Evertz, 2001; Randi Korn Associates, 2006; Beth Redmond Jones, 2007.
27. Fields, personal interview, 2006.
28. Cantsee, personal interview, 2006.
29. Cantsee, personal interview, 2006.
30. Holly, personal interview, 2006.
31. Murphy, personal interview, 2006.
32. Timbimboo Madsen, personal interview, 2006.
33. Tom, personal interview, 2006.
34. Cesspooch, personal interview, 2013.

CHAPTER 5

Taking Responsibility for Museum History and Legacy

Promoting Change in Collections Management

> People working on behalf of museums commissioned, bought, and outright stole from Indigenous communities in a frenzy of collecting from "vanishing" cultures at the end of the nineteenth century. This has led to a great distrust of museums, which are rightfully seen as part of a larger imperial project, places exclusively for non-Natives. The image of the museum as a place that holds your ancestors' bodies and epitomizes the cultural theft of your people is not a place that you are likely to visit.[1]

COLLECTING ARTIFACTS and material culture lies at the core of museum practice; collecting and caring for objects and archival materials is one of the things that define museums. It is this practice that creates wide-ranging emotions in Native people. Museums hold cultural patrimony that, at times, has been robbed from tribes, which resulted in cultural loss. On the other hand, because of preservation practices, when museums grant unrestricted access to tribal members to learn from collections, elements of traditional arts can be resurrected. The Native American Graves Protection and Repartition Act (NAGPRA) altered museum collections and practices in numerous ways—the legal implications of which are covered in many other publications. However, there are ethical considerations for collections management as well, which impact best practices for interpreting Native culture. Collections access, care, and documentation can be one of the most significant sources of stress between museums and Native communities, but it can also provide opportunities for the most meaningful relationships and transformational changes for both the museum and Native people.

Background on Collecting Practices in the United States

It is important to understand the history of collecting Native material culture in the United States to fully understand why Native communities are sometimes reluctant to work with museums. As part of the research phase of learning about the museum's history, which was outlined in chapter 2, a thorough analysis of the collecting practices of the museum is required. Many museums in the United States have Native American collections, whether interpreting Native history and art is part of the mission or not. Native American objects appear in natural history museums, which between the mid-1800s and early 1900s interpreted indigenous cultures as part of the natural world. Historical societies often have archaeological collections from the region and likely baskets, pottery, or other forms of material culture as well. Art, science, and children's museums may at times also have Native American collections. Museums must understand how they came to have these collections and learn more about the collecting practices that brought the items to the museum.

Early Collecting

Ruth Phillips, among others, has written extensively about collecting practices from the time of European contact through the present. There were lots of motivations for collecting Native objects; early collectors took home souvenirs of beauty and also items that highlighted the differences between European and Native cultures. Collections were assembled for research and preservation, and to excite visitors with visions of the "exotic."

In the entrance hall to Thomas Jefferson's homes, Monticello and Poplar Forest, were displays of "Indian relics," including deerskin dresses, painted buffalo robes, and a cradleboard.[2] Soon after the Lewis and Clark expedition, the idea of an America that stretched from the Atlantic to the Pacific took hold, and Native people were seen as obstacles to this goal. As more and more Native communities were removed from their home territories, died from disease and warfare, or were forced through assimilation programs, Americans began to believe that American Indians would vanish from the landscape.

In light of this idea, painters and collectors swept into Indian communities to document customs and cultures before they were gone. Along with it came the fields of anthropology and archaeology, to formally study these cultures before they were lost forever. Museums and private collectors purchased objects or asked to have items sent back from collectors in the field. "The museum collectors spread out over the continent in ever-widening circles. As their letters show, their goal was to fill in the boxes of a kind of imagined chart of object types—a cross between a map and a periodic table—in which all functional categories would be represented for all tribal groups."[3]

Native people at times served as collectors and brokers for collectors, to help target specific types of items museums and private collectors were looking for. "Christina Kreps has noted, the assertion that 'non-western people are not concerned with the collection, care, and preservation of their cultural property . . . has frequently been used to justify the collection (or some would say plunder) and retention of non-western people's cultural property in museums.'"[4]

The removal of both everyday and ceremonial objects from Native communities created, in some ways, a self-fulfilling prophecy, in which tribal members no longer had examples of religious and daily cultural expressions to pass on to future generations, thereby making these items more rare, and traditions more difficult to continue. "In the late nineteenth and early twentieth century, concerned with physical survival and the continuance of their communities and ways of life, Native people often entrusted museums with items of significant cultural patrimony for fear they would end up in private collections. In these cases, Native people did not receive them back for many years, if at all."[5]

Collectors and the types of objects they collected had other impacts on tribal communities. Collectors often looked for examples of the "oldest" objects—those that exhibited no or little influence from Europeans—as a means of representing "pure" Native cultural expressions. In fact, the idea that there was a time when "outsiders" did not influence Native communities is fantasy, but often remains a lens through which non-Native people value and evaluate Native art. Phillips proposes one possible reason for the emphasis on older, "traditional" materials and artifacts: "objects that displayed the traces of aboriginal peoples' negotiation of Western artistic and economic systems had to be excluded from formal programs of collecting and exhibiting in order to support the standard museum representation of Native Americans as other, as marginalized and as pre-modern."[6]

Native material culture has always evolved and changed based on changes in available resources, and inspiration from exposure to new ideas and cultures. This is what makes a living culture, not one that is static. As Native communities relied more on American economic systems and were less able to sustain themselves though traditional methods, art became an important economic tool. In addition, the thriving contemporary Native art scene in North America today is evidence that many Native artists are inspired by traditional materials, techniques, and values but also incorporate new and innovative ways of expressing these ideas and identities. This is a continuation of the ways in which Native people have long used art as a form of cultural expression and economic sustainability.

Collecting Historic and Tourist Art

In the northeast, tourism was an important industry by the mid-1800s, with wealthy people traveling from industrialized cities like Boston and New York, to more scenic and pastoral destinations, like the coast of Maine and Niagara Falls. Native people from these areas would also travel to these locations, with inventory to sell as souvenirs and keepsakes. Iroquois artists were well known for a characteristic style of beading used on wall hangings, purses, and other "whimseys." They sold baskets, postcards, carvings, and many other handmade items. Along the coast of Maine, in the American Southwest, parts of California, and other places, Native people adapted traditional items made for daily life into buyable art forms that appealed to tourists. These art forms changed over time with market demands but are still no less important as cultural expressions. The importance of these items for the economic survival of Indian families could sometimes impacted traditional social structures because many of the artists were women who were selling their work and therefore could become the primary income source for the family. Or conversely, the impact could reinforce traditional social structures, in the case of matrilineal societies, and challenge it in the case of patrilineal societies. Phillips argues that they also "illuminate histories of interaction between Native and non-Native, an inter-cultural story that the ethnologist's paradigm of race and exclusive ethnicity could not easily narrate."[7]

As important as tourist items were for the economic and cultural survival of tribal communities, they were not considered important to museum collectors, who often overlooked them in their collecting efforts. "The exclusions were as significant as the inclusions. The problem, of course, was that collections that excluded the interchangeable, mass-produced commodities that by 1912 were being used by *all* North Americans could represent only imagined, not actual, lifestyles."[8]

Knowing Your Collecting History

All this is to say that by embarking on a self-study of the collecting practices of a museum, it is important to consider how the collection was started. A gap analysis of the collection is an important tool that can help museum staff start to understand what stories the museum can tell through its collections and what stories are missing. To conduct a gap analysis, collections staff work with consultants and experts in the type of collection being analyzed to create a list of objects in the collection. From this list, duplicate items are identified and categorized based on provenance and condition. The list is then compared with the mission of the museum, and ideally, the interpretive plan. It is from this comparison that gaps in the collections can be determined. Once the gaps are identified, collecting practices can focus on acquiring objects to fill those gaps. An alternative to directly acquiring new objects to fill gaps in the collection is to identify other organizations or communities that have access to the identified items and build a relationship such that it is possible to borrow objects needed for exhibits.

Consider stories that are not currently being told, either by other museums in the area or with the same collecting focus, or stories that represent gaps in local school curriculum. Work with tribal advisors to identify gaps in the stories they would like to see told about their communities, and ask for their help to fill these gaps as opportunities are presented. Regardless of a museum's NAGPRA compliance, the gap analysis opens a window for deeper collaboration with Native historians, cultural leaders, Tribal Historic Preservation Officers (THPOs), and artists. There are many objects that may not fall under NAGPRA but still have importance to tribes. A museum has the opportunity to work with artists to make reproductions of collections items, either to keep in the museum or for use in the community. Amanda Cobb points out that sometimes "it is not the object itself, but the community's use of an object that lends it its significance."[9]

Transforming Collecting into Collaboration

When a museum is transparent with its collection scope, policies, preservation methods, and collecting history, it presents new opportunities to work with Native people, which are collaborations that can benefit both the museum and tribal communities. Because so much of the material cultural history of tribal communities has been removed and stored in museums, granting access to tribal members can be critically important to cultural retention and revitalization efforts. There are many examples of museums opening collections for tours with elders and language students, enabling them to reconnect with historic and pre-contact objects and archival collections. Artists wanting to learn more about traditional designs, materials, or techniques rely on collections as teaching tools, as do linguists working with historic recordings and documents.

The art of building birchbark canoes was nearly lost in the Northeast, but through thorough research of museum collections and archival materials about canoe making, the art has been revitalized. Birchbark canoe builder and basketmaker David Moses Bridges, Passamaquoddy, credits working with collections in many museums with improving his basketmaking techniques. Through close examination of historic bark baskets, David came to understand the technique for preventing the bark from bending over time, thus warping the basket. Because of positive interactions with museums, specifically the Abbe Museum, located in his tribal territory, David has begun to transfer some of his own work to the Abbe, including sketches and journals that document his growth as an artist and his artistic process. These are collections that will be extremely valuable to future artists.

A brief example of the benefits of collaboration between museums and a tribe can be found from the Zuni of New Mexico. Before, and since, the passage of NAGPRA, the staff at the Zuni Cultural Center, *A:shiwi A:wan Ulohnanne*, spent time in museums around the world collecting information about Zuni objects held in collections, correcting misinformation and working with collection staff to enhance understanding about the items cared for in these collections. Jim Enote, Director of the Cultural Center, said because each museum he worked with used a different system for cataloging the collections, they lacked interoperability, preventing the Zuni from building relationships and connections between disparate objects in different museums. In other words, if one museum had a collection of images, and another museum had additional images from that set, or an object in one of the images, there was no way to link them together for research or reference purposes. At the same time, collections were becoming digitized, and rather than "jump on the digitization bandwagon, we wanted to show we were capable of contributing to the field, to be part of shaping and engaging how digital media works with our community."[10] *A:shiwi A:wan Ulohnanne* worked with software designers to create *Amidolanne*, which translates to "rainbow" from Zuni. *Amidolanne* takes information from the collections management software of participating museums and drops it into this software, which is housed and maintained by the Zuni within their community. It functions like a web portal, and the Zuni can review information and make corrections or additions to the database, and then determine if they want to share that information, or keep it private in the community. "This is one way to address the asymmetry of power that museums have had over items that contain knowledge, and give source communities the ability to see items and write commentary, and decide for themselves, to keep that knowledge, or share it."[11]

Museums can benefit from relationships with tribal historians, artists, linguists, and elders in many ways. Opening collections to tribal members has filled in gaps and corrected assumptions made by museum staff and collectors in the past. For example, in northern California, several tribes make hats out of basket materials. The hats are made to rest with the opening down, opposite of how a basket made for storage or decoration is made. When Native people from this region visit collections storage areas, they often see these hats stored upside down, as baskets. By sharing with museum staff the purpose and design of these baskets, and the need to store them rim down, tribal members are helping to educate museum staff and also improve preservation and storage methods for the hats.

During collections tours, tribal members have also identified artists and family members who created items in collections, improving provenance and enhancing the research value of those items. Tribal members have also identified mistakes in collections records and filled in gaps. The benefits of tribal access to collections cannot be overstated, but museum staff need to be cautious as well. There are many objects in collections that will bring up painful memories; create mental, spiritual, or physical health risks; or feelings of anger at the cultural loss the collections represent. Be sensitive to tribal members working with objects, check in to see how they are feeling, and if they need a break or want to stop. Try not to surprise tribal people working with collections, but share in advance as much information as you can about the collection, the objects, and their history.

Storage and Object Care Procedures

By researching the history of a museum's collections, museum staff will learn more about the types of objects they care for and more about the history of acquisition. Take the time to consider how certain objects are stored and their proximity to other collections. If Native people are spending time in collections, be sure to consider the range of emotions and possible reactions they will experience when spending time with the collection, and be respectful of their needs and feelings. Certain tribal values link objects and people in very personal, intimate ways, which are not shared by western values. Understand, that for some Native people, connecting with an object may be reconnecting with a long lost loved one, and the experience will be emotional.

A personal experience with two museums in Oklahoma will help illustrate this point. While at a museum conference with the Association of Tribal Archives, Libraries, and Museums (ATALM), two off-site tours were offered through regional museums. Both museums were general museums that had extensive collections of Native art and artifacts in addition to many other types of objects. At the first tour, we met collections staff and a curator, who took small groups into collections storage to see the facility and get a behind-the-scenes look at the breadth of the collection. As many collections staff do, they showed us highlights from the collection. Unfortunately, one of the "highlights" (from the curator's point of view) was a human remain that had been made into jewelry. The reaction from the group was devastating to observe. Pain, anger, betrayal, and sickness washed over the entire group, with many leaving the space altogether. The collections were stored on open shelves, and as people moved away to process their feelings they found other items made from human remains visible in open storage. Thankfully, the jewelry made from human remains was removed and placed back in storage for the remaining tours, but the damage was done and the group had a difficult time enjoying the rest of the museum.

The tour group then went to the second museum, with a collecting scope and organizational size similar to the first museum. When the group walked in, the curator greeted us at the door, and to the full group she shared that there were human remains in collections. She then went on to explain that the remains had been removed from general collections and were stored in a private, dark room, representing a symbolic burial, until they could be repatriated. No one on the tour would have access to that room, but we would be near it during the collections tour. She concluded by saying that anyone uncomfortable being in proximity to the remains could choose to skip the collections tour and explore the galleries instead. I do not know if anyone skipped the tour, which is one of the elements that made this experience so much more respectful than the first: no one had to explain his or her feelings or share with the group, and they did not need to ask permission to skip this experience. The respect accorded the group made the experience at this second museum much more enjoyable.

Caring Guidelines

For many types of collections, especially ceremonial objects, there are guidelines by the tribe for how best to care for an object. Amy Lonetree points out that "it is true that the museum as a specific concept is foreign to Native peoples; however, caring for and cherishing cultural patrimony is not, regardless of commonly held scholarly views on that matter. . . . Caring for cultural property is hardly a new idea for Native people, and indeed may exist at the center of many cultures."[12] The trust and partnerships established through earlier processes will help when consulting with Native advisors on the best ways to care for culturally sensitive objects in the collections.

Human remains, burial goods, sacred or ceremonial objects, or objects of cultural patrimony may have special considerations in regard to how they are cared for, who has access to them, and at what times. The needs of the objects will vary widely based on the tribe and the type of object. Build on the good relationships already established, or take this opportunity to create new relationships by inviting Native people in to learn about the collection and teach museum staff about the collection and how to care for it based on cultural values. Ask if there are special considerations for the storage and care of the objects. Some examples of considerations can include restrictions for women, who may not be able to touch some objects at all or are restricted at certain times of the month, or perhaps only certain members of the tribe can access an object. Some objects are considered living and need to be "fed" and have access to water periodically.

In the early 1990s the Clarke Museum in northern California had an extensive collection of ceremonial blades made from obsidian. As part of the ceremonial tradition for the local tribes, the blades were buried underground until they were needed for ceremony. The museum symbolically buried the blades, even while on exhibit, with a fine layer of clean dirt. The purpose has been included as part of the educational experience for visitors and tribal members alike. It may be that not all restrictions and considerations can be accommodated, but sharing the information and working together to make special arrangements and agreements can resolve many issues and establish greater trust

Conclusion

Tribal communities are living cultures that require specific ceremonial items to continue traditions. Many of these items had been removed from the communities and housed in museums through various processes mentioned. It must be acknowledged that living, healthy communities are more important than the preservation of objects representing those cultures. "This adaptation of the museum—to expand the preservation goals beyond the preservation of artifacts to the preservation of a living culture—is an essential component of the Indigenization of the mainstream museum model."[13]

There are a few examples of museums loaning ceremonial objects from the collections to source tribes for use, which are then returned after the ceremonies have been completed. In this way, the museum and tribes can work together to preserve both the historic objects in collections but also living cultures reliant on those objects. There are examples of museums caring for Native collections on behalf of the tribe, until they can build a cultural center and care for these items themselves. Access and use restrictions can be negotiated and understood as those opportunities come available. These partnerships represent strong trust relationships between a museum and tribal community.

It cannot be stressed enough that each tribe is different and will have different expectations and needs for how their items are cared for in collections. There will also be differing opinions within the tribe. Keeping open lines of communication, being honest and forthright about everything the museum has done, is doing, or wants to do in the future, and listening, will help all involved work toward an appropriate outcome.

Because of the emphasis on collecting objects that represented early Native life—before European influence—objects that were culturally representative of early life or the most beautiful, unique, or scared objects, many museum collections of Native material have large gaps in historic and contemporary Native culture. It is just as important to collect and interpret modern Native cultural expressions as the historic. If a museum follows an exhibit and collecting practice that is chronological, most likely representation of Native people stops soon after the early 1900s. By not collecting contemporary objects and interpreting the contemporary lives of Native people, museums segregate Native history as being apart from American history. It represents Native peoples as "other," not integrated into the daily life of modern America. This segregation serves many purposes related to how Americans like to tell the story of our history, but it primarily serves to reinforce stereotypes of Native people as living in the past. It suggests that the Native story is only interesting or worth telling when they are "other" and apart from the mainstream.

CASE STUDY: THE ABBE MUSEUM

SEEKING A COLLABORATIVE FUTURE THROUGH DECOLONIZATION

Darren Ranco, Ph.D., Chair of Native American Programs, University of Maine; and Julia Clark, Director of Collections and Interpretation

The object of this essay is to look at the history of the Robert Abbe Museum of Stone Age Antiquities in Bar Harbor, Maine, in light of changes made to the organization based on recent theories and practices of decolonization. Founded in 1928 as a "trailside curiosity," the museum has recently begun a decolonization initiative to engender greater collaboration with the Wabanaki Tribes in Maine.

A Humble Beginning and a "Vanished Race"

> Introducing the collection of Stone Age Implements, Lafayette National Park [now Acadia National Park] will stand for the epitome of the beauty and wonder of nature on the Eastern Continental coast; but the complete drama of its history will be lacking in interest after its geology and consummate beauty of living things have been studied; if we do not gather together and consecrate in a Museum these Stone Age implements of agriculture and war which have been the indestructible evidence of a vanished race.[14]

When the Abbe Museum (originally called the Lafayette National Park Museum, then the Robert Abbe Museum of Stone Age Antiquities) first started out, founder Dr. Robert Abbe's interests rested entirely with archaeological collections. In 1927, as Abbe was getting his museum up and running, he stated "In working out this problem of exhibiting only one limited phase of the antiquity of the Stone Age, I have consistently set a goal—never to enlarge this collection into a general museum but fix indelibly a fact of incontrovertible history on the minds of the large and rapidly growing traveling public"[15] (Figure 5.1).

Furthermore, Abbe explicitly stated that the museum would not include anything about historic or contemporary Native Americans: "With recent Indian life, however, we will not concern ourselves"[16] His *Aims and Ideals* provide additional explanation of why this was the case, when he refers to the artifacts he had gathered as the "indestructible evidence of a vanished race." He simply did not see a connection between the artifacts and living Native Americans, which is especially significant because there was an annual summer encampment of Wabanaki people in Bar Harbor with which Abbe would have been plenty familiar.

Abbe believed that all of the archaeological artifacts were from a different race, now extinct. At that time, the understanding of both the relative and absolute ages of archaeological sites and artifacts was limited, and archaeologists were just beginning to consider the relationship between the two best-known types of archaeological sites in Maine—shell middens and "Red Paint" burials.

Abbe was familiar with museums such as the American Museum of Natural History, George Heye's Museum of the American Indian, and the Peabody Museum at Harvard,

Figure 5.1. The interior of the Abbe Museum ca. 1930. Photo courtesy of the Abbe Museum.

and although he saw these as important resources, he wanted to create something different, a "permanent classic 'one show' historic incident in the path of the 'maddening crowd' and to make it as perfect as possible." As he continues, "large museums covering all archaeology repel the usual visitor by consuming too much time and bringing fatigue."[17]

The Abbe Museum's first nonarchaeological collections were added in 1930 with gifts from Mary Cabot Wheelwright, among others. These included baskets, birchbark pieces, tools, and beadwork. Although the museum and the donors of the time appear to be acknowledging a connection of some sort between the archaeological record and artifacts from current (or at least eighteenth and nineteenth century) Native American communities in the region, there was a strong focus on finding the oldest, least "corrupted" examples of material culture. This was common across North American museums collecting Native American material at the time and wrapped up in colonial perspectives and bias regarding twentieth-century Native people.

What is somewhat distinctive about the nonarchaeological collections at the Abbe as opposed to other museums in the late nineteenth and early twentieth century is that from the early years until the present, the bulk of its collections are objects made for sale, not objects made for use by Native people in their everyday lives. This has meant that the Abbe's collections do not include items that were essential to Native American communities at the time and illegally or unethically removed from these communities. As a result, during the process of implementing NAGPRA requirements, the Abbe Museum and consulted tribes did not identify any sacred objects or objects of cultural patrimony in the museum's nonarchaeological collections.

As far as we can tell from limited records, there was no direct involvement of Native people in the acquisition, management, or interpretation of Abbe collections until the 1970s. In this decade, the museum began to have Wabanaki artisans on site doing demonstrations of things like basketmaking.

Wabanaki is a collective term that encompasses the four federally recognized tribes in Maine—the Micmac, Maliseet, Penobscot, and Passamaquoddy—and the Abenaki, who are federally recognized in Canada and have state recognition in Vermont. In 2010, the Native American population in Maine was just less than 10,000. It is important to note that although the Abbe Museum has, and continues to build, strong positive relationships with tribes in Maine, this has not always been the case and is not currently true of the relations between the tribes and some other museums in the state and region.

On Collecting: Placing the Abbe in a Colonial Context

A number of scholars have described the colonial origins of museums as they relate to the collection of Native American artifacts, peoples, and identities. Phillips identifies the four elements/actors that came together in the second part of the nineteenth century and beginning of the twentieth century to produce most ethnographic collections and how they create, and maintain, colonial narratives of erasure. For Phillips, these actors were (1) the ethnographic collector, (2) the Native agent collector, (3) the rare art collector, and (4) the tourist.[18] Working together, these interests inscribed ethnographic collections as "privileging the past over present"[19] in a way that ignored any "Native system of aesthetics, use and value."[20] Conceptually, searching for "old" and "authentic" pieces and displaying them as the most representational pieces of a culture "prevented other kinds of authenticity . . . from being recognized."[21] Thus, in symbolic terms, "we can interpret colonial museum representations as simple narratives of geographical displacement of the other by European colonization."[22] In the case of the Abbe, the fact that the collection was not being connected to modern Native people in the area, or their ancestors, helped the displacement narrative even further—it allowed the Euro-American viewer the pleasure of gazing at the primitive without any possible sense that they were responsible for the actual displacement of an indigenous people.

In Maine, the narrative of archaeological discontinuity continues through the present day. Most of Maine's current archaeological community and museums with archaeological collections continue to have different perspectives on the pre-European history of the Wabanaki from those held by the Wabanaki themselves. Archaeologists (most, but not all) feel that archaeological evidence shows a substantial discontinuity at the end of the Archaic Period (about 4000–3800 years ago), and because of this, argue that Native Americans living in Maine today are not culturally affiliated with archaeological materials and sites that predate 3800 B.P. In other words, archaeologists argue that today's Wabanaki can only trace their ancestry back 3800 years in Maine. Even more importantly, many archaeologists who have worked in Maine support the cultural affiliation of objects found only in the last 1000 years to contemporary Wabanaki communities.

Many Wabanaki (including those on the intertribal Wabanaki Repatriation Committee), on the other hand, believe that they have been here from the beginning, and that most, if not all, pre-European sites and artifacts in Maine were created by their ancestors. These divergent perspectives have critical implications for the management, care, and control of archaeological collections. This is especially important because many of the archaeological collections in museums that date to the Archaic Period in Maine are burial objects—a suite of stone tools placed in graves—in which the human skeletal remains are not preserved because of soil conditions.

Collections Planning and Tribal Partnerships

An essential aspect of good collections management is collections planning. Most museums have limited resources for collections: limited space, limited funds for the care of collections, and limited staff time to manage and provide access to collections. The Abbe is currently working with a collecting plan created in 2005 and will be building an updated collecting plan based on a new interpretive plan currently in the works. As part of the planning process, the Abbe has been reviewing its current collection for its strengths and weaknesses, based on input from tribal communities and the Abbe's new decolonization initiative.

Most of the Abbe's current collection, through both purchase and donations, continues to be of objects made for sale, so-called "tourist art" and fine contemporary Wabanaki art and crafts. The biggest gap in the collection is objects that support in-depth interpretation of Wabanaki daily life, recent history, and current issues. Some interesting exceptions include a beaded wedding dress made by Susan Thompson, Penobscot, in the early 2000s, casino referendum signs and bumper stickers, Penobscot chief Barry Dana's running shoes, and Maliseet artist Rose Tomah's mother-in-law's pickle/bread bowl. If visitors are going to get a full, rich picture about the Wabanaki, the Abbe needs to be able to tell a wide variety of stories that provide plenty of context for understanding the diversity, complexity, and adaptability of the tribes and communities and ensure that visitors leave with no doubt that there are Native people in Maine today.

As part of its colonial past, the Abbe, along with many other Native American museums, must deal with its past focus on identifying and collecting the oldest, least-westernized (therefore thought to be more "authentic") objects and ignoring the fact that Native American people and their material culture have always adapted to changing environments, be they natural or cultural. Ignoring the results of that adaptation feeds into the misconception that "real" Indians are a thing of the past. It is important to have collections that reflect the change and adaptation that has been such a central part of Native American life since the arrival of the first Europeans, as a companion to the change and adaptation reflected in the archaeological collections.

As part of the process of overcoming these past biases, the Abbe must evaluate how its collection can help interpret stories or themes important to Wabanaki people. The Abbe's contemporary basket collection can help tell the story of the importance of basketmaking to the economic survival of the Wabanaki and the carrying on of traditions. This is also reflected in the Abbe's contemporary birchbark, beadwork, and wood carving.

Furthermore, the Abbe is relatively well equipped to tell stories around the importance of tourist art in the eighteenth- to twentieth-century life of the Wabanaki (see Phillips, *Trading Identities*), but has fewer objects outside basketry, such as beadwork, toys, souvenirs, and postcards. This gap was revealed during the creation of a recent exhibit, *Indians & Rusticators*, which was filled by borrowing pieces from other museums and private collections.

In some instances, identifying other collections from which a museum can borrow is an important part of collections planning; if a museum that can easily collaborate with another has strong collections in an area in which the first museum has a weakness, perhaps it makes the most sense to plan on borrowing from that institution (or private collection) as opposed to adding (purchasing) items. This is especially important for nontribal Native American museums, in which competition (real or perceived) with tribal museums is something to be avoided.

Another major area for improvement at the Abbe is documenting Wabanaki traditional knowledge about the Abbe's historic and contemporary collections, through language, oral tradition, and Wabanaki perspectives in first-person voice on the role of such objects in their lives and culture. The work being done by tribal museums in this regard may serve as a good model to improve the Abbe's practices.

To overcome previous colonial biases about collecting, the Abbe can also do more to involve Wabanaki people in decisions about what we should be collecting and cooperatively developing strategies to do so. An important component of this is not competing with tribal museums. Currently there is one Wabanaki member on the Abbe's collections committee, and it would be beneficial to increase Native representation on this committee. The Abbe should also consult the recently established Native Advisory Council to gain input and perspectives on large or particularly thorny issues about collections. This might include issues about determining who is a Wabanaki artist or craftsperson (and thus whose work we should be collecting) or ongoing issues about the repatriation of archaeological material.

The emphasis on collecting pieces made by, and important to, Wabanaki people would be a departure for the Abbe, which has spent most of its years developing collections of archaeological and older historic materials. In 1973, the museum acquired its first pieces made by living Wabanaki craftspeople, which was an assortment of baskets purchased on behalf of the Abbe by C. Gardner Lane from the Passamaquoddy Basket Co-op and other Passamaquoddy basketmakers. We know the makers of some of these baskets; but for others, an individual creator is not recorded. Of some interest is the fact that at least one unfinished basket was acquired clearly with the intention of showing something of the process.

Seven years later in 1980, two more contemporary work baskets were purchased from Maliseet basketmakers, James and Audrey Tomah. More direct involvement of Wabanaki people is evidenced by a gift made in 1983 from Barbara Francis, curator, on behalf of the Penobscot Nation Museum, of a basket by Eunice Crowley and a miniature totem pole by Stan Neptune. During the 1980s, the Abbe also began to build relationships with Wabanaki artisans through the purchase of pieces to sell in the Abbe museum shop, and this continues to be a key interface with contemporary Wabanaki artists and craftspeople.

Archaeological collections present a whole other set of concerns, challenges, and opportunities. The Abbe's earliest collections were made by individual collectors or avocational archaeologists in the Mount Desert Island area and were either donated to or purchased by Abbe as he worked to build a collection focusing on the Stone Age, concentrated on the island and its immediate environs. A small subset of the pre-1928 collections were excavated by Warren K. Moorehead and a crew from Phillips Academy and donated to the collection for the planned museum. These early collections were split between coastal shell middens and so-called "Red Paint People" burial sites.[23] Moorehead was one of Abbe's "professional" advisors as he worked to build a "scientific" collection of Stone Age artifacts.

In 1928, the museum began conducting or sponsoring excavations at sites around Frenchman Bay. Collections also continued to be donated by individuals, and small collections were donated by other archaeologists/institutions, such as Phillips Academy (the R. S. Peabody Museum) and the Maine State Museum.

A dual focus on shell middens and burials reflected the focus of archaeology in Maine at the time, and there was likely no Wabanaki involvement in collecting or excavations. This was a time when the relationship between living Native people and the archaeological record was just beginning to be considered and consensus was building among archaeologists that the shell middens were created by the "Algonquin race," who were the Native people present when Europeans first arrived, but that the "Red Paint People" were an earlier race, now extinct, and not related to contemporary Native Americans. Amazingly, this view still holds sway in much of the archaeological community in Maine and the Northeast, albeit with a more refined terminology and framework. This has ongoing impact on how archaeological collections are managed, and how NAGPRA has been applied in Maine.

During the 1990s, the Abbe Museum went through the process of implementing NAGPRA requirements and repatriated all human remains in the Abbe's collections. No artifacts were repatriated because none of the human remains had associated grave goods. Additional human remains that came into the Abbe's possession through the transfer of a collection from another institution were also repatriated to the Wabanaki. The Abbe Museum still holds a substantial collection of unassociated (not associated with preserved human remains) burial objects from the Archaic Period in the Abbe's collections. To date, the Abbe has not received a repatriation request in regard to these collections but is aware that several other institutions are in the process of addressing more recent repatriation requests for Archaic Period material. Information about the Abbe's collections was provided to the Wabanaki Repatriation Committee as part of the Abbe's original NAGPRA inventory, and we may receive a claim at some point in the future. The Abbe made the decision sometime in the 1980s not to exhibit or otherwise publicly display artifacts attributed to burial contexts and to follow handling guidelines provided by the Wabanaki Repatriation Committee during the repatriation of human remains. These include restrictions on the consumption of alcohol and the menstrual cycle of individuals involved in the care and handling of the collections.

The Abbe has accepted donated collections that appear to be burial assemblages in recent years. The intention has been to provide appropriate care for these sensitive collections, and in some cases, to keep them out of the artifact market. In addition, the Abbe Museum does not (1) purchase archaeological material or (2) assign monetary value to archaeological collections. As an institution, the Abbe believes it is unethical to sell archaeological artifacts from Native American sites, and these two policies reinforce that stance.

The Abbe Grows Up: From Trailside Curiosity to Downtown Museum

The passage of NAGPRA in 1990 symbolized not just a change in the law in terms of collection practices but a changing culture within Museums and Native American activism as it relates to artifacts, heritage protection, and museum practices in general. Beginning in the 1980s, museums started to address issues such as identity, representation and voice, and issues of title that arose from Nazi seizures of Jewish collections during World War II. Racial and cultural minorities who had been previously left out of decisions in museums that held their cultural patrimony were also demanding to be heard and have their perspectives heard in exhibits, collecting practices, and programs at museums. This is true of Wabanaki people as well. Members of Wabanaki communities participated in all of the major Native American activist movements in the 1970s and 1980s and continue to be engaged in these movements in both the United States and Canada. All of the five tribes have developed language and heritage programs, with each of the Passamaquoddy communities and Penobscot Nation managing collections in tribal museums. Tribal orientation and programs focused on heritage protection have also gradually increased since 1980 in Maine, with the passage of the Maine Indian Claims Settlement Act in that year, as well as with federal recognition of the Penobscot Nation (1978), Passamaquoddy Tribe (1978), Houlton Band of Maliseet Indians (1980), and Aroostook Band of Micmacs (1991).

As the Abbe began to implement NAGPRA in the 1990s, the museum was also undertaking a major capital campaign to open a downtown Bar Harbor location. This new, larger location would provide many more opportunities for the museum to explore collection and exhibit practices that better represent contemporary ideas about the representation, voices, and identities of Native Americans. The creation of the much larger downtown location in 2001, which immediately became the primary location for Abbe exhibits, programs, and staff, changed the nature and dynamics of the museum itself. No longer a small, trailside curiosity, the Abbe took on a more robust and diverse set of programs and exhibits.

The new location also created opportunities to engage tribal communities in collaborative exhibit development—emphasizing tribal points of view and perspectives in ways never attempted at the original trailside location. The creation of the *Four Mollys* exhibit in 2001 showed the possibilities of collaborative exhibit-making in a way that was previously unimaginable in a typical ethnographic, colonial space. Representatives from all of the tribes were part of designing, organizing, and implementing the exhibit (Figure 5.2). This also led, in the short term, to more representation from the Wabanaki Nations on the Board.

Immediately after the *Four Mollys* exhibit and the opening of the downtown location, the museum world suffered a downturn in funding with the events of 9/11 (the downtown location officially opened at the end of September 2001). This clearly impacted the momentum of collaboration with Native peoples in terms of exhibit development and other issues and slowed the ability of the Abbe to develop its identity as a museum committed to a diverse set of rotating exhibits and programs and ultimately away from an archaeological orientation. Adding to the changes the Abbe was undergoing, archaeologist Diane Kopec, director of the museum through the transition from trailside museum to the downtown location, retired in 2006.

Figure 5.2. The Wabanaki women who served as advisors for the *Four Mollys: Women of the Dawn* exhibit celebrate the exhibit opening in 2002. Photo by Peter Travers, courtesy of the Abbe Museum.

The Move toward Decolonization

The combination of funding concerns, staff transitions, and a still-emerging identity led to a number of fits and starts around the Abbe museum's direction after Kopec's retirement. The board, concerned about the financial potential of a museum devoted to only local Native American populations, hired Kopec's replacement to expand beyond the emphasis on local Wabanaki Tribes and seek funding from new places. The shift was not feasible or supported by the staff, Wabanaki, or museum stakeholders and Kopec's replacement left within two years. For more than a year, the Abbe was without a director/CEO, and this further slowed the development and direction of the museum. During this time period, with a focus seemingly oriented toward tribes and people outside of Maine, and even some non-Native content, some of the goodwill and connections with the Wabanaki that defined the *Four Mollys* exhibit and other programs were lost. A couple Wabanaki people left or were termed-off the board and only co-author Ranco remained as the lone Native American board member. As is often the case in such situations with limited funding, the issues of Native American collaboration became less of a priority because they do not usually bring in immediate funds.

Figure 5.3. The Abbe Museum Native Advisory Council at its inaugural meeting in 2012. Photo courtesy of the Abbe Museum

Eventually, the Board hired Cinnamon Catlin-Legutko in 2009. Catlin-Legutko had previously been the director of the General Lew Wallace Study and Museum in Crawfordsville, Indiana, where she led the organization to the National Medal for Museum Service in 2008. With great skill in managing small museums, Cinnamon has had great success in working with the board and staff to reorient the mission toward local Native American communities and collaboration in ways that have national and international appeal. In 2012, the museum formalized a Native Advisory Council, with representatives from each of the five Wabanaki Tribal governments in Maine (Figure 5.3).

Within a year of Catlin-Legutko's hiring, the Abbe unveiled a new mission statement to "inspire new learning about the Wabanaki Nations with every visit." This created great appeal and a clear focus for the board, the staff, and the Native and non-Native audiences that the museum serves. As programs and exhibits became oriented toward this clearer mission, the board and staff became more engaged. Under Catlin-Legutko's leadership, a process to "decolonize" the museum formalized a process that in many ways began with NAGPRA and the *Four Mollys* exhibit over the previous twenty years.

For the Abbe, the interest in decolonization is as much an ethical practice—to build collaborations with Native peoples—as it is in developing and exhibiting interesting, unique, and compelling stories with universal human appeal; this finally fulfills the educational mission of the museum set out by its founder. To do this, true collaboration and trust must be built with Native peoples and communities. This does, and will, take a long time, yet the Abbe is committed to become a national leader in this regard.

Inspired by Ho-Chunk scholar Lonetree's extremely incisive 2009 essay, "Museums as Sites of Decolonization: Truth Telling in National and Tribal Museums,"[24] the Abbe formed the Decolonization Initiate (DCI) in 2012, which a task force that makes recommendations to the staff and board on issues of collaboration, truth-telling in the museum, the primacy of first-person Native voice, and the process of implementing and sustaining this practice in perpetuity. The choice to use the term *decolonize* in and of itself sets a purposeful tone that shows the museum's deep institutional commitment to right wrongs, work in collaboration, and tell true stories of Native American experiences before and after European contact, from both Native and non-Native points of view.

Lonetree's article points out very clearly that one of the primary problems for Native American museums (especially nontribal ones) is that those who walk into them have "no clear and coherent understanding of colonialism and its ongoing effects."[25] Furthermore, "the first step toward decolonization is to question the legitimacy of colonization."[26] Presenting visitors with programs and exhibits that do this is a difficult but worthwhile challenge to a nontribal Native American museum and eventually opens up new and important avenues for exhibits, collaboration, collections management, and governance. The DCI has taken up the challenge posed by Lonetree in three areas as a way to develop and evaluate decolonized exhibits: (1) Does it tell "hard truths" about colonization? (2) Does it privilege Native American stories/narratives, and (3) Was it done in collaboration with Native peoples?

Conclusion

The move toward decolonization is a pathway for the Abbe Museum to correct the colonial elements of the original mission of the museum, while preserving the deeply important educational mission. Abbe's purposeful separation of local Native Americans from the "stone-age antiquities" represented in the original collections served a (probably) unwitting colonial purpose to make contemporary tribal claims for land and rights much more difficult and clearly represented museum practices of the time period. That said, Abbe's interest in Maine's prehistoric past serves as an important educational jumping-off point for visitors to gain a true understanding of Native American experiences in the region now known as Maine—both before and after the arrival of Europeans. Tribal participation in this process not only advances a truer understanding of their experience but also has the possibility of advancing the heritage protection and other issues they face in lieu of colonial legacies in anthropology and history.

Notes

1. Kristina Ackley, "Tsiʔniyukwalihoʔta, the Oneida Nation Museum Creating a Space for Haudenosaunee Kinship and Identity" in *Contesting Knowledge: Museums and Indigenous*

Perspectives, edited by Susan Sleeper-Smith (Lincoln: University of Nebraska Press, 2009), 265.

2. David Hurst Thomas, *Skull Wars: Kennewick Man, Archaeology, and the Battle for Native American Identity*, (New York: Basic Books, , 2000), 29.
3. Ruth Phillips, "Why Not Tourist Art? Significant Silences in Native American Museum Representations," in *After Colonialism: Imperial Histories and Postcolonial Displacements*, edited by Gyan Prakash (Princeton, NJ: Princeton University Press, 1995), 105.
4. Amanda J. Cobb, "The National Museum of the American Indian as Cultural Sovereignty," in *The National Museum of the American Indian Critical Conversations*, edited by Amy Lonetree and Amanda J. Cobb (Lincoln: University of Nebraska Press, 2008), 335–336.
5. Ackley, "Tsi?niyukwaliho?ta," 265.
6. Phillips, "Why Not Tourist Art?" 100.
7. Phillips, "Why Not Tourist Art?" 112.
8. Phillips, "Why Not Tourist Art?" 106.
9. Cobb, "The National Museum of the American Indian as Cultural Sovereignty," 346.
10. Jim Enote, personal conversation, November 5, 2013.
11. Jim Enote, personal conversation, November 5, 2013.
12. Cobb, "The National Museum of the American Indian as Cultural Sovereignty," 335–336.
13. Ackley, "Tsi?niyukwaliho?ta," 276.
14. Robert Abbe, "Aims and Ideals," Abbe Museum archives, 1927.
15. Abbe, "Aims and Ideals."
16. Robert Abbe, "The Stone Age Period of Civilization in Evidence About the Maine Coast Adjacent to Lafayette National Park," *Bar Harbor Times*, ca. 1927).
17. Abbe, "Aims and Ideals."
18. Phillips, "Why Not Tourist Art?" 95–125.
19. Phillips, "Why Not Tourist Art?" 110.
20. Phillips, "Why Not Tourist Art?" 108.
21. Phillips, "Why Not Tourist Art?" 112.
22. Phillips, "Why Not Tourist Art?" 114.
23. Two types of archaeological sites were familiar to people on or near the Maine coast in the early twentieth century: large clamshell middens located on the coast and large cemetery sites located primarily on rivers and lakes. The types of artifacts from the two sites were different, and early archaeologists, without the benefit of radiocarbon dating, did not know if these two types of sites represented two different groups living side by side or represented change over time. We now know that the large burial sites with their distinctive ground stone tools predate the large majority of the shell middens, showing change over time.
24. Amy Lonetree, "Museums as Sites of Decolonization: Truth Telling in National and Tribal Museums," in *Contesting Knowledge: Museums and Indigenous Perspectives*, edited by Susan Sleeper-Smith (Lincoln: University of Nebraska Press, 2009), 322–337.
25. Lonetree, "Museums as Sites of Decolonization," 322.
26. Lonetree, "Museums as Sites of Decolonization," 323.

CHAPTER 6

Establishing Tribal Partners in Education and Public Programs

> The most powerful moments that happen . . . occur when non-Native visitors encounter Native interpreters, when the face-to-face nature of this encounter brings conflicting myths and histories into direct proximity.[1]

EXHIBITS, PUBLIC PROGRAMS, and education are the most obvious and public ways that museums interpret Native culture. The process of working with Native people to create exhibits, share authority, and develop content has been discussed already, but public programs and educational experiences for schools offers another, and different, opportunity to partner with Native advisors. Patricia Pierce Erikson argues that "No matter what museum you look at, the exhibition galleries are only one expression of the institution's identity."[2] Most museums offer some level of educational programming to accompany exhibits and to enhance visitor experience. Museums with Native American collections have the opportunity to work with Native artists, historians, linguists, and others to create unique and memorable learning experiences for visitors.

Working with Native Interpreters

Creating public programs that focus on Native history, culture, and contemporary issues can further the impact of an exhibit experience, reach different audiences, and explore topics not covered in the written interpretation. Although there are many highly qualified non-Native people capable of sharing information about Native culture with visitors, the most meaningful, and lasting interactions take place between Native demonstrators, speakers, and interpreters and non-Native visitors. Native people bring a different perspective, a level of personal experience, that an outsider will never understand. "Native interpreters infuse their work with highly charged, personal meanings that challenge on several levels the stereotypes expected by visitors. These messages are not always the same as the official ones of the site, or the ones they are supposed to communicate."[3] Be open to the experiences and knowledge that Native people want to share with visitors. Each interaction and experience will be different, depending on the presenter and the visitor.

There is a long, at times, uncomfortable history of Native people being on display in museums, zoos, vaudeville shows, and fairs. Starting with the early Europeans, Native people were taken to Europe and toured as curiosities, meeting royalty and displayed as "other." During the late 1800s and into the early 1900s, Native people were still seen as wild, yet also unthreatening and interesting. With the notion of the vanishing Indian, Wild West shows toured with Native troupes hoping to capitalize on the fascination of seeing the last of this noble race. Native people dressed in costume and performed for audiences, sometimes wearing traditional clothing and performing ceremonies and celebrations specific to their culture. At other times, Native people were playing a role to satisfy the expectations of the audience, including wearing the clothing and performing the traditions of another tribe or something made up for the purpose of the performance.

Daniel Francis points out that:

> by the end of the nineteenth century, Native people were perceived as things of the past, especially as the "taming" of the western frontier seemed complete. . . . The Performing Indian was a tame Indian, one who had lost the power to frighten anyone. Fairs and exhibitions represented a manipulation of nostalgia. They allowed non-Natives to admire aspects of aboriginal culture, safely located in the past, without confronting the problems of contemporary Native people. Frozen as they were in an historical stereotype, Performing Indians invoked a bygone era.[4]

Not all performances were stereotypes, and there were certainly Native performers who folded in elements of their language and traditions, and many who toured and performed independently. Performers like Molly Spotted Elk, Princess Watahwaso, Frank "Big Thunder" Loring, and Henry Red Eagle, all combined elements of their specific cultural traditions with the pageantry and regalia of other tribes, specifically those from the Great Plains. The goal was to combine truth with fiction, to give visitors what they wanted and expected to see (feathered war bonnets, rain dances, and tipis), but also a glimpse of the unique elements of their specific culture.

The enduring legacy of this performance history is that non-Native people still overwhelmingly expect to see Native educators, artists, and presenters in traditional regalia, rather than modern dress. Non-Native visitors are also more comfortable talking to Native presenters about the past, and about material culture, rather then contemporary issues and culture or uncomfortable or traumatic events of the past. Rather than continue offering programs about the past, or programs created by non-Native people assuming what would be important or interesting, working with Native presenters can open whole new avenues for reaching audiences. "Native peoples have indicated a strong desire to participate in the creation and delivery of representations about their peoples, and there are important reasons that they should do so."[5]

Like with everything discussed thus far, there is no formula for creating educational and public programs with Native partners. The important thing is to start by being receptive to different ideas and perspectives. "I think that the work of Native interpreters, and the implications of adding Native perspectives, has posed more fundamental challenges to historic sites than expected, and I think that some sites have begun to stall in their process of revision because they cannot reconcile different cultural perspectives on the past, cannot meet the very different agendas of tribal communities, and are uncertain how to proceed."[6]

There are elements in every Native culture that are acceptable to share with outsiders, and other elements that are not. Some presenters will want to wear traditional regalia, others will not; for some presentations regalia is appropriate, for others it is not. Some presenters will want to smudge or offer a greeting or prayer in their Native language, others will not. Sometimes one presenter is comfortable talking about a topic, tradition, or artistic technique, and another presenter from the same tribe is not comfortable talking about those things. Each presenter will create a different experience for the visitors, so ask up front about their individual style of presentation, what the expectations and needs are, and if there is anything he or she would like you to know beforehand. Let the presenter lead the decision process for each specific event because it will change over time, depending on the audience or as the presenter changes.

Native communities understand the importance of sharing information about their history and culture, and often value non-Native partners in this process because it is understood that neither Native communities nor museums have the resources needed to embark on this mission alone. Authors M. Scott Momaday and Vine Deloria, Jr., write about the challenges of balancing scientific perspectives with oral history but, "in different ways, Momaday and Deloria both urge Indians to take back control over their own heritage because in doing so, they will also gain control over their own identities."[7] This is at the core of all partnerships with Native communities, and creating opportunities to explore multiple ways of knowing about the world and the past and sharing authority to tell different stories are ways that museums can support this process.

Before embarking on a program or series, it is helpful to begin by working with Native advisors, or with the presenters being considered, to create the themes, identify additional presenters, and establish learning objectives, or the goals for the program. Consider what visitors should leave knowing more about, what themes will support the mission of the museum, or the objective of the exhibit the program is associated with. Is it important that visitors learn about the materials and process needed to make a specific craft? Challenge the group to think deeper, asking why that is important? Maybe that information is how the presenter starts a conversation with a visitor, but the real goal is to share the economic and cultural importance of the craft to the community today. Ask Native advisors what they want to share about their culture. Make sure to create programs that represent the diversity, depth, and uniqueness of the community. Oral history and craft programs are popular, but represent a limited scope of the culture. Look for contemporary artists and authors who want to share their work today, perhaps linking it to the traditions and values of the community, perhaps not. It is also important to present programs on topics that are more difficult, such as sovereignty, jurisdiction, environmental management, and economic development. These topics help visitors understand the sovereign status of the Nation and also break stereotypes about Native people. In addition, it can help improve relations between tribal and nontribal communities.

Public programs create new opportunities for museums to support modern Native communities. Artists benefit from meeting visitors to the museum by increasing awareness, appreciation, and understanding about their work. This can have a ripple effect into the community, as demand for the craft increases, or artists earn more for their work as visitors understand and appreciate the time and labor involved in the craft. Over time, the popularity of a craft will attract apprentices, who will in turn become artists, thereby ensuring that the tradition is passed on to future generations. Asking master crafters to bring their apprentices along is a great way to encourage this relationship and to start developing presentation skills in the apprentices.

Working with youth groups is also an important way to help recognize the value of maintaining and passing on traditions. Many tribes have youth drumming and dancing groups, which can perform at exhibit openings, public programs, or as part of a larger event, and youth presenters are always popular with visitors. Hosting kids' workshops and programs with youth demonstrators and exhibits that include children's artwork can encourage young artists, and it "prepares children to step up when it's their turn to carry on these cultural teachings."[8]

Once museum staff and Native program advisors establish what the purpose of the program is and what visitors will take away from the experience, then that information can become the foundation for booking additional or future presenters. With this information clearly stated, the stylistic differences between presenters, or the specific information that is shared by individual presenters, will be less of a concern, as long as the goals are being met. For example, if a museum offered a series of programs on basket weaving, a goal could be that visitors will come to understand the historic and cultural importance of basketmaking to the economic and cultural survival of a community. With that goal in mind, each presenter could speak about the aspect of basketmaking with which they are most comfortable—harvesting, teaching the next generation, economic independence, etc. Visitors would get a different, personal experience from each weaver, but the overall educational message would be the same. By allowing presenters the freedom to create programs with museum staff and to speak to their expertise and comfort level, the presenters will be more comfortable with visitors, thereby creating a more meaningful and memorable experience. "The implications for sites that wish to interpret the history of a particular Native group is that the group may well want to talk more about their worldview and less about the 'things' to which its culture has often been reduced. 'We are more than arrowheads' is how Marie Battiste (Mi'kmaq) put it."[9]

What Visitors Bring to the Experience

Native presenters will each bring their own unique experiences, knowledge about the history and culture of the community, presentation style, and perspective to public programs. Visitors will also bring their own expectations, experiences, and knowledge to interactions with Native presenters. "Many visitors exhibit automatic, stereotyped responses: children break into

Hollywood-Indian war whoops (and) parents make jokes about scalping. . . . The positive messages (the staff and site managers) wish to communicate about Native peoples, often translate for visitors into the generic frontier drama of good White guys and savage Indians."[10]

Be prepared for visitors to say the most ignorant, silly, or even racist things about and to Native interpreters. Most experienced Native presenters are used to this, unfortunately, and have developed amazing skills for how to gently correct visitors and change the course of the conversation. From personal experience, visitors can be nervous around Native people at first, and many have never met a Native American before. Visitors can be uncertain about how to start interacting with the presenter and may try to "break the ice" with a joke. To help make the initial interaction easier, especially during drop-in style demonstrations, have some kind of object, art, craft, or hands-on activity that visitors can ask about. Even with this, visitors will often still make inappropriate jokes. Another way to help visitors meet presenters in a respectful way is to have a member of the museum staff on site during the program, introducing the speaker and the program to visitors as they drop in. This has the additional benefit of pulling in more visitors to the program, and also supporting the presenter, especially if he or she is busy with other visitors.

Rather than be caught off guard by visitor comments and questions that might offend the presenter or other visitors, take some time before the presentation to talk to the presenter about this possibility. Ask if they have had any similar experiences, and how they have handled it in the past. Ask the presenter how they would like it handled during the presentation—at what point does the presenter feel intervention is appropriate, if they would like to personally address the visitor, or if they would be more comfortable with a museum staff member stepping in? No one wants a confrontation with a visitor, so instead of challenging a visitor who says something inappropriate, gently correct the misinformation. Saying something along the lines of "You know, a lot of people think that, but actually . . ." is an easy way to change the course of a conversation without alienating anyone. It is important that the exchange be positive, kind, and informative, so that visitors feel safe to ask questions, especially if they know little about the culture.

Museum staff and Native presenters cannot be experts on all of the myths and stereotypes that visitors will bring to the interaction, but some advance planning will help a lot and cover most of the basics. Take some time to research local news coverage of Native issues to get a sense for what people have been seeing about these topics. There are ongoing topics covered in the media, like hunting and fishing rights, casinos, and local celebrations, but there will be other issues as well, like taxation, identity, or veterans. Be aware of the history of the issues, and sort through the fact versus fiction of each to be prepared to help visitors think critically about what they think they know about Native people and history. "Historical interpretation at its essence is about getting visitors to learn and to rethink. . . . Freeman Tilden stated that 'the chief aim of interpretation is not instruction, but provocation.'"[11]

School Programs

Creating school programs for students based on the mission of the museum, collections, exhibits, and state education standards has become standard museum practice. Museums with Native collections may have school programs about the Native people who lived in the region prior to European contact, based primarily on archaeological evidence and historical accounts. It is impossible to know how many museums have created school programs that include historic and contemporary Native history and culture or were created in partnership with Native people leading the development process, but this should be standard practice.

Leading up to this section, we have focused on authority sharing, strong collaborations with Native people, and direct Native voice in exhibits and programs as best practices for interpreting Native history and culture. Museum school programs are an area in which direct interaction between Native educators and schoolchildren is difficult for a museum to coordinate and likely outside of the control of the museum. Unless there is a Native educator on staff (and he or she chooses to reveal his or her identity to the students as part of the program), it is most likely that a non-Native person will be teaching museum educational programs about Native history and culture. This is where creativity, the strength of existing partnerships with Native people, and balance will be most helpful. Museum educators should not speak "for" Native people, but they need to speak about Native cultures in a way that is respectful and shares accurate history and contemporary life of Native people with students.

Begin by looking at any existing school programs that discuss Native history or culture. Do an internal audit of the program(s) to see if it is accurate, if the information stops at the time of European contact or with the early history of the non-Native community, and if the programs include anything about modern Native life and culture.

Once the weaknesses have been identified and corrected, invite Native advisors to review the programs and make suggestions for changes, additions, and new programs. Be prepared to compensate them for this time because as expert advisors the knowledge and perspective they can provide is invaluable to the process.

> Those following the Indigenous paradigm adhere to research methodology that includes producing scholarship that serves Native communities; following Indigenous communities' protocols when conducting research; rigorously interrogating existing scholarship and calling out the "anti-Indigenous concept and language" embedded in existing literature; incorporating Indigenous language, such as place-names, names of people, and proper nouns; and finally, privileging Indigenous sources and perspectives over non-Indigenous ones.[12]

Working with advisors on the revision or creation of a school program can be different from working with advisors for exhibits and public programs. Because a non-Native educator is most likely going to be presenting the program, direct Native voice is not as effective or realistic. As a result, the education staff at the museum needs to be equally involved in developing the content of the programs to ensure that they are fully prepared to present the information. One option is to interview Native people about specific aspects of the subject being presented to school groups. For example, if the museum offers a program about Native life prior to European contact, interview Native advisors about oral history that tells how the community came into being. Ask how men, women, and children might spend the days, how they would prepare for a storm, or what the community might do for fun and leisure time. Try and balance the information presented to be a mixture of all the different ways of knowing about the past: archaeology, oral history, primary source materials from Native Americans and early Europeans, and other sources. One of the goals of education is to teach children to be critical thinkers. By incorporating, and talking about, different ways of knowing about the past, and the strengths and weaknesses of each, children can leave with better skills to analyze information from different sources.

Schoolchildren will come to the program with stereotypes of Native people as well. Trends in media will determine much of these, including film, books, and web sites. Attitudes that they hear from home will also inform students' understanding of Native people. There have long been dual representations of Native people— as either savage or ecological; the "bad" Indians were portrayed in film and books as violent and subhuman, whereas the "good" Indians were friendly and concerned for the environment and the welfare of all.

> Alternatively, they represent the stereotype we might call the "Eco-savage," and/or the "Egalitarian Savage," a new variant of an old pattern of using Native peoples as foils for European society: the Noble Savage redux. Even these superficially positive images are Othering, though, and fail to displace the controlling relations between Native peoples and the dominant society in historical narratives.[13]

Students will have encountered all of these different portrayals of Native people and more and bring that with them to museum programs. As with adults, it is helpful to be aware of what children are learning about Native culture, to be prepared for and address any inappropriate comments. Creating a safe environment for questions is just as important for children as it is for the general pubic.

Review state educational standards and assessments and incorporate that into the development of school programs. Most, if not all, states have standards that include teaching about Native American history and culture. Some states, like Maine and Montana, require this for all grade levels, whereas other states only require it at certain grade levels. Align program activities, outcomes, pre- and post-visit activities, and content with these standards. With the increased focus on assessment and testing, teachers do not have as much time for professional development, to work with new content, or for field trips. Think creatively about the standards museum programs will meet, and try to incorporate multiple disciplines into program development. There are many ways Native specific programs can meet math, science, economic, and civics and government standards. Teachers will be better able to justify the time if a school program is well thought out and clearly linked to state standards.

Beyond working with school groups, museums have the opportunity to work with teachers, to support their professional development and improve their access to resources and content knowledge. Teacher workshops are one way to provide direct Native voice and perspective by crafting a professional development experience for teachers to learn from Native scholars, artists, and educators. Museums can work with regional education administrators to be approved to offer contact hours for teachers for workshops. Short after-school workshops can be focused on a specific topic, or day-long workshops can offer deeper learning and the opportunity to try new lessons created or distributed by the museum or tribe, or to create new lessons on their own. Objects are primary sources of information, and teacher's benefit from working with collections and artists during professional development programs. Showing teachers the value of the museum, its collections, and the thoroughness of the programs is one of the most successful ways of bringing new school groups to the museum.

> The real voices that matter, though, are those of the interpreters themselves. While the stories suggested by artifacts are crucial, it is dangerous to let them remain implicit, for . . . they can be "read" by visitors as easily within misinformed narratives as they can within intended ones. Neither sites nor their furnishings speak for themselves: they are spoken about by interpreters and visitors.[14]

By providing teachers the opportunity to meet and learn from Native presenters, it will grow the network of educators teaching responsibly about Native history and culture.

Hands-on Activities

Exhibits, public programs, and school programs often include hands-on activities to engage visitors with multiple ways of learning. These are important and often fun elements in any museum program, but when working with Native content, museum staff developing hands-on activities must be cautious. There are interactive activities that support and advance stereotypes or that appropriate cultural and religious elements of Native communities. Playing dress up is often popular in children's areas in museums, but it is not appropriate to encourage children to dress up and pretend to be Native. Native American is not a profession, like other dress-up activities. Although dressing up in period costume from the frontier or settlement time is often understood as pretending to be part of the past, this is not true for dressing as a Native person from the same time period. Because representations of Native people so often take place in the past, this activity becomes an extension of colonization and stereotypes, rather than one that promotes understanding. Similarly, making drums available for use as an interactive can be problematic.

When developing interactive elements, the trust relationship already established with tribal representatives and communities will be vital. Tribal representatives must be involved in the identification and development of interactive activities. It is in this area in which differences within communities and between communities is often evident. For some communities, it is acceptable to have an activity that represents the different techniques for weaving a basket, believing that visitors develop greater understanding and respect for the tradition by trying a simple version of the skill. For other communities, this activity has been criticized as oversimplifying the process. Both thoughts are correct, and museum staff need to balance the educational value with the risks involved in allowing visitors to play with Indian arts, craft, and culture.

There are many activities that can be created in partnership with tribal communities that are fun, interactive, and educational, while respecting Native concerns about privacy, appropriation, and authenticity. Compare and contrast activities can be fun and informative, or linking the past with the present through games is another way to integrate education about stereotypes into interactive elements of an exhibit or program. The key when developing an interactive component is communication with the tribal community, identification of clear outcomes for the activity, and observation and evaluation of visitors interacting with the activity. Watch and make sure that visitors are not coming up with inappropriate ways of engaging with the activity, and if they are, change it. Evaluation is an important element in all museum work and is certainly true for interactive elements.

Conclusion

Working with Native advisors to create public and school programs continues the practice of authority sharing, enriches the experience of visitors, and helps to correct misinformation and stereotypes about Native people. The fact that museums have a history of helping advance misinformation about Indian culture, stereotypes, and messages of colonization makes it all the more important for public and school programs to focus on correcting this past. "What a great irony that [museums and historic sites] inextricably linked to the colonization process are also the sites where the difficult aspects of our history can and must be most clearly and forcefully told. Only by doing so can we address the legacies of historical unresolved grief."[15]

As places for informal learning, where hands-on, objects-based experiences can engage visitors of all ages in multiple ways of understanding, museums are natural centers to foster critical thinking. Rather than teaching facts, dates, and statistics, museum education can inspire people to continue their learning when they leave the museum. Holistic interpretation led by Native people often places more value on oral history and contemporary life, giving the museum visitor a unique and unexpected experience. Quoting from Perry, Roberts, Morrisey, and Silverman:

> While visitors may have a primary social agenda, they also want and expect to learn something new, have their curiosity piqued, see something they've never seen before.... By listening to visitors, museum professionals have realized that they are not—and should not be—in the business of teaching. Instead they are in the business of creating environments that facilitate the construction of appropriate meanings, that engage people in the stuff of science, art, and history.[16]

By breaking the mold of how Native history and culture have been interpreted, to crafting a new model that includes collaboration at all levels, museums can engage with visitors in a whole new way.

CASE STUDY: PORTLAND ART MUSEUM: *OBJECT STORIES*

CONNECTING COLLECTIONS WITH COMMUNITIES

Deana D. Dartt, PhD, Curator of Native American Art, Portland Art Museum

Michael Murawski, PhD, Director of Education & Public Programs, Portland Art Museum

In 1989, the Portland Art Museum brought together a group of about twenty people to discuss the museum's Rasmussen Collection of Northwest Coast Native American Art. Gathering in the museum's basement, the group included museum staff, art experts, anthropologist and historian James Clifford, and a group of Tlingit elders accompanied by translators. Objects from the collection were brought out one by one, presented to the elders for comment with the expectation that they would tell museum staff about how each object was used or by whom they were made. Instead, as Clifford recounts, "the objects in the Rasmussen Collection, focus for the consultation, were left—or so it seemed to me—at the margin. For long periods no one paid any attention to them. Stories and songs took center stage"[17]

Rather than providing historical details and context that could be easily converted into research files or didactic labels, the session brought forth voices, songs, dances, ongoing stories, and lived experiences that challenged the museum with alternative perspectives on these objects, as well as a potential way of decentering the museum's authorial voice. Instead of envisioning ways to bring these voices and stories into dialogue with the collection, the museum bid the group goodbye and archived the audio and video footage of the consultation. Little, if any, of the content acquired was used to inform catalogue entries or interpretive labels, primarily because no one on staff quite understood what they had witnessed.

Twenty-five years after these "conversations in the basement," the Portland Art Museum is actively working to re-address many of the issues around interpreting its Native American collection, including the hire of a Native curator whose research focus is the substantive integration of diverse voices and community perspectives into curatorial and educational practice.[18] This case study will focus on two recent projects piloted within the museum's *Object Stories* initiative, which is a partnership with the Native American Youth Association (NAYA) Family Center to connect Native youth voices with the collection, and an artist-led project that has gathered stories from Yup'ik tribe members in Bethel, Alaska.

The Collection

The Portland Art Museum stewards more than fifty-two thousand works of art, nearly five thousand of which comprise the Native American collection. With objects dating from pre-European contact to the present, the collection features important works from nearly every tribal group in North America, with especially strong representation from tribes in the Northwest coastal region and the Columbia Plateau. Anchored by the world-renowned Axel Rasmussen Collection of Northwest Coast Native American Art and the encyclopedic

Elizabeth Cole Butler Collection, the Museum's Native American art collection is the single most-visited aspect of the museum's permanent collection—and the most popular destination for K–12 students visiting the museum from schools in Oregon and Washington.

Established in 1948, the Native American collection has been on continuous view since 1949, when the Portland Art Museum was the first museum to dedicate permanent gallery space to the exhibition of Native American objects as works of art rather than as anthropological artifacts. In addition to these major collections of historic Native American art, the museum has acquired works by contemporary Native American artists including Rick Bartow, Lillian Pitt, James Lavadour, Marvin Oliver, Gail Tremblay, Marcus Amerman, and Marie Watt. These works reveal the vitality and continuance of Native culture and suggest new bridges for research between scholars and contemporary Native artists.

Object Stories

Framed by larger challenges facing museums in the twenty-first century, the Portland Art Museum has been involved in a broader process of rethinking how it relates to its public audience and exploring strategies to be more relevant to its community. In doing so, museum staff have uncovered that both the museum and the public need catalysts for active participation, personal reflection, and meaningful ways to discover and rediscover works of art in the collection. It was out of this ongoing thinking that the *Object Stories* project was born.

Since its inception, the *Object Stories* concept has evolved into a comprehensive educational platform for engaging audiences, forging collaborations, and bringing community voices into the process of interpreting the collection. By capturing, honoring, and sharing participants' stories, the *Object Stories* project aims to demystify the museum, making it more accessible, welcoming, and meaningful to a greater diversity of communities while continuing to highlight the inherent relationship between people and things. This initiative also allows the museum to explore how new media and other technological innovations can contribute to more genuinely inclusive engagement with audiences and communities.

Launched in March 2011, *Object Stories* invites visitors to share stories about an object, whether personally owned or part of the museum's collection. Comprised of a recording booth, website, and interactive gallery space, *Object Stories* collects oral and written testimonies and provides arts education opportunities to diverse communities through targeted outreach and partnerships. Current visitors to the museum's *Object Stories* gallery encounter a central table with two large interactive touch screens that enable them to browse, search, and listen to more than one thousand collected stories about personal objects and artworks from the collection. On the surrounding walls, guests find a rotating selection of museum objects that have been the subject of recent stories, often related to a larger theme or special exhibition. Elizabeth Wood and Kiersten Latham describe *Object Stories* in their recent book *The Objects of Experience: Transforming Visitor-Object Encounters in Museums*:

> The recorded stories reinforce the personal experience that people have with objects. In the same way that personal objects evoke powerful feelings and experiences—clearly demonstrated through the stories the museum's visitors have shared—the stories about museum objects hold a high level of personal connection.[19]

Figure 6.1. *Object Stories* gallery on the Lower Level of the Portland Art Museum. Photo by Cody Maxwell

By the end of 2011, the Portland Art Museum had extended *Object Stories* into an Institute of Museum and Library Services (IMLS)-funded three-year partnership with area middle schools that involved in-depth teacher professional development, artist residencies, and multiple visits to the museum that culminated in students recording their own personal "object stories." More recently, the museum has focused on recording personal stories related to objects from the museum's collection, creating an alternative to the museum's institutional voice by adding the voices of community members to in-gallery interpretation. During 2013, *Object Stories* projects brought the Portland Art Museum into an international partnership with the Museo Nacional de San Carlos in Mexico City; a more locally focused partnership with the NAYA Family Center; and an artist-led project that has gathered stories from Yup'ik tribe members in Bethel, Alaska. These latter two projects will be described in detail.

The internal process of developing and implementing *Object Stories* has encouraged meaningful and sustained collaboration between education and curatorial departments, the growth of new partnerships with community organizations, and the confidence to experiment with a formative approach to programming that aims to be inclusive of the voices, stories, memories, and experiences of the museum's audience and community. Scholars have questioned how a museum's voice might be changed from monovocal (single voice, often an institutional "voice from nowhere") to a more polyvocal (many voices, without much sense of hierarchy).[20]

> In this scenario, museums are encouraged to give up some of their control and their authorial voice to allow the public or specific communities to speak for themselves and be heard in a public space (Mason et al., 2013, 164).

The *Object Stories* projects discussed in this case study have begun to bring museum staff and community members into new forms of collaboration as we work together to explore ways to bring polyvocality and shared authority into museum practice.

The Community

Portland has the ninth largest Native American population in the United States, with nearly sixty thousand single-race or multiracial Native Americans living in the Portland Metro area. Portland's Multnomah County rests on traditional village sites of the Multnomah, Kathlamet, Clackamas, bands of Chinook, Tualatin Kalapuya, Molalla, and many other tribes who made their homes along the Columbia River, and the current Native American population includes descendents from approximately four hundred tribes. This diverse and growing community, however, is largely underserved and faces deep economic and educational challenges. Native people in the Portland metropolitan area count disproportionately among the urban poor, experiencing the highest rates of homelessness, poverty, and unemployment of all ethnic groups. Native Americans constitute 24 percent of all children in foster care in Multnomah County, Oregon; only 37 percent of Native American high school students living in Portland graduate on time; and among those graduating, only 54 percent enter higher education.[21]

Native American service organizations address these inequalities and create a space for Native Americans to reconnect with each other, their ceremonies, and their cultures, yet the Native American community remains largely disconnected from the museums that house many of their cultural artifacts. Research has shown that engagement with cultural objects affirms Native American youth's sense of identity, which has been linked to better performance in school and a broad range of other personal positive effects. Framed by these larger concerns, the Portland Art Museum has begun to rethink how it can actively emphasize a multiplicity of perspectives and forge connections with the contemporary experiences, contexts, and practices of Native artists and their communities.

Connecting Collections with Communities

Listening to the Ancestors

Beginning in the fall of 2013, the Portland Art Museum launched a partnership with the NAYA Family Center's Early College Academy and worked with the museum's existing community-based interpretive platform of *Object Stories* to bring these Native voices into the galleries. Each participating student was asked to choose an object from the museum's Native American collection that resonated with them in some meaningful way, conduct

Figure 6.2. NAYA Early College Academy students studying objects from the Portland Art Museum's Native American collection. Photo by Deana Dartt

research on the work, and then record their personal narratives about that artwork. NAYA students visited the museum on multiple occasions during the project, not only spending time in the galleries but also getting to know curatorial and education staff and learning more about the inner working of a public art museum. During one visit, the students were able to closely study their selected objects, many of which had not been on view in the museum's galleries.

After more than two months of work between the museum and the NAYA students, the stories created for this project were exhibited along with the students' selected artworks in the *Object Stories* gallery located in a prominent location in the museum's lower level. Each of the student's stories can also be accessed through the project's website at www.objectstories.org (by entering "NAYA" in the Search field), allowing these stories to reach wider audiences through a digital format. Each story shares information about the object from the collection and makes meaningful personal connections to the storyteller's life. The story excerpt here, relating to a Beaded Bag (ca. 1900) created by an unknown Pitt River artist, shows the types of connections that participating students were able to make through this process of shared learning with the museum:

> Cherokee, my tribe, also has similar bags. They are used for the same things. This relation warms my heart because it makes me feel closer to my ancestors. The bag also reminds me of my hairpiece through the color patterns and designs. My mom got this for me at a pow-wow. She is also the main reason I know about my heritage. I now know more about myself and where I come from. My mom is my hero. Working on this project just makes me so proud to be native, and I appreciate how passionate natives are about their culture and what they believe in.

In addition to the student stories, three Oregon Native mentors—including NAYA Cultural Arts Instructors and an elder from the Native community—recorded stories connected to objects in the collection as part of this project. The museum installed these stories directly into the Native American collection galleries, allowing visitors to use a new iPad listening station to access these stories adjacent to where the objects were on view. This represented the first instance when the museum brought the *Object Stories* project into its permanent collection galleries as a way to actively work with the Native community to co-create knowledge and understanding about these objects, connect contemporary voices and lived experiences with these objects, and present these stories in a public way for visitors to engage with them as part of their museum experience. The experiences and stories that are part of this project work toward offering alternative perspectives on works of Native American art in the collection, provide an avenue for understanding historic Native art in the context of the modern urban, Indian experience, and begin to incorporate stronger Native voice in interpretive efforts.[22]

Yup'ik Stories

Early in 2013, education and curatorial staff from the Portland Art Museum met with Alaskan artist and photographer Katie Basile to explore the possibility of recording "object stories" with Yup'ik community members during one of her trips to Bethel, Alaska. Originally from Southwest Alaska, Basile was involved in several media arts and storytelling projects with the rural community in and around Bethel. At the same time, the museum was prototyping a new iPad app that would allow *Object Stories* content to be recorded outside of the museum, using the iPad device to capture audio and photographs through a new mobile platform. For her first trip to Alaska as part of this project, Basile used one of the museum's iPads to record a series of personal object stories from Yup'ik tribal elders, artists, and youth. During a return visit to Bethel, Basile brought images of Yup'ik masks and dance wands from the Portland Art Museum's collection to gather connected stories from Yup'ik elders and artists. The story excerpt is from Alaska Native mask artist Drew Michael, telling a story connecting his own artistic process to the Yup'ik masks in the museum's collection:

Figure 6.3. Screen shot from *Object Stories* told by Alaska Native artist Drew Michael. Photo by Katie Basile

> [W]hen I look at masks, I try to understand somebody else's perspective. When I have masks that I'm creating, I typically am telling a story from my place and my environment and my time. . . . To me, the most beautiful thing is looking at a mask and seeing how the story is portrayed and expressed using the materials that are from your environment. With my work, I'm using materials that are around me, and that sometimes includes going to the store [laughs]—it doesn't mean that I have to go to the beach or the woods to find the material.

As part of the larger initiative to generate knowledge and interpretive resources with the Native community in the public spaces of the museum, these Yup'ik stories have been exhibited in the Arctic Native American Art gallery through an additional iPad listening station adjacent to their related objects. Bringing together personal object stories and collection-based stories, the museum is offering visitors a layered and nuanced learning experience as the Yup'ik tribe members share their personal and cultural perspectives. Furthermore, through this prototype *Object Stories* project with Basile, the museum has begun to build a new model for interpretation that brings Native artists into the core of planning, collaborating, creating, and editing content within our Native American Art collection, an interpretive model the Portland Art Museum will be building and extending in the upcoming years with its collection and exhibitions.

Taking the notion of collaboration and consultation a step further than past efforts, Basile as a community-based researcher, and the use of the iPad app within the community allowed for organic, first-person narratives to emerge about objects currently held in the museum without the need to involve the museum—its staff and perceived authority—in the conversation. The community in Bethel was made aware of the Portland Art Museum holdings, shown the collection online, and alerted young artists such as Drew Michael (Yup'ik) of the accessibility of the museum's Alaska Native collection for research.

The content developed during the pilot Yup'ik storytelling project has proven so meaningful that the Museum plans to expand the model to targeted communities, beginning locally—with Oregon tribal groups—using the connections and expertise of the Native artists to record community members' stories as part of the *Object Stories* initiative. First-person narratives by origin community members will then be available to museum visitors through iPads, online collections, and other digital strategies in addition to the more conventional interpretation in the galleries.

In addition to the decentralization of authority, the *Object Stories* platform allows for an emphasis on individual Native voices, unsettling notions of "community voice," which stereotypes Native people and assumes a "Native" way of being, thinking, and art-making process and philosophy. In this model, individual artists—rural, urban, young, and old—are able to express what is important to them from within—but not necessarily defined by—their tribal history and culture.

Steps Forward

As we move forward, we have identified some limits to our work at the Portland Art Museum and where we need to ground ourselves before we continue. We realize the need to talk to visitors and Native community members to explore responses to these stories and notions of "alternative" voices in the galleries. We learned that in an effort to collect and share meaningful Native community stories, we will need to have Native participants serve as editors for the stories themselves. During editing of both the NAYA and Yup'ik stories, we used internal education staff and realized the shortcoming of this approach. We also realized that confining the NAYA youth to an object search that only included Native American art was also limiting. It was only after they had chosen their objects that it occurred to us how interesting it would have been to offer up the entire collection for their perusal.

In 1989—pre-Native American Graves Protection and Repatriation Act—the Portland Art Museum was bold and progressive, if only somewhat ethnocentric, to secure National Endowment for the Humanities funding to bring Tlingit tribal members to the museum to help the institution tell a more meaningful story of the ancestral objects as it redesigned the Native American galleries. Although motives were pure and collaboration was intended, the museum stood between the objects and the stories. The museum attempted to serve as the bridge for the visitors between the ancestral object and the descendent storyteller. However, the stories and objects out of context required much more interpretation than time allowed, so the tapes sat idle with museum staff clueless about any connection to the collection the stories were intended to enliven. Museums have continued to mediate the connection between story and object. We hope to step out of the way.

Object Stories allows people to bring story back to objects disembodied from their cultures and their people. We hope that through this work we can reunite the ancestors with (while introducing museum visitors to) the energy, language, and living traditions of Native people. Best practices, such as the ones highlighted in this case study and volume, have the power to transform museums from "sites where knowledge is transmitted to passive audiences to potential forums or contact zones where new voices and visibilities are raised and new knowledge(s) actively constructed."[23] In many ways, the *Object Stories* platform challenges the museum, its audiences, and its communities to consider the complex types of exchange and dialogue that might occur with its collections beyond the traditional experience of passive, didactic looking. This platform is enabling us to facilitate, and then share, the dialogue between the maker and the viewer and through a process of shared authority and unmediated connection may transform the way museums see, use, and present Native American art.

Works Cited

Clifford, J. (1997). "Museums as Contact Zones," in *Routes: Travel and Translation in the Late Twentieth Century* (edited by J. Clifford). Cambridge, MA: Harvard University Press.

Curry-Stevens, A., Cross-Hemmer, A., & Coalition of Communities of Color. (2011). *The Native American Community in Multnomah County: An Unsettling Profile*. Portland, OR: Portland State University.

Dartt-Newton, D. (2009). "Negotiating the Master Narrative: Museums and the Indian/Californio Community of California's Central Coast." PhD dissertation, University of Oregon.

Golding, V. (2013). "Collaborative Museums: Curators, Communities, Collections," in *Museums and Communities: Curators, Collections, and Collaboration* (edited by V. Golding & W. Modes). London: Bloomsbury.

Golding, V. (2009). *Learning at the Museum Frontiers: Identity, Race, and Power*. Surrey: Ashgate.

Hutchison, M., & Collins, L. (2009). "Translations: Experiments in Dialogic Representation of Cultural Diversity in Three Museum Sound Installations." *Museums and Society* 7(2): 92–109.

Lynch, B., & Alberti, S. (2010). "Legacies of Prejudice: History, Race, and Co-production in the Museum." *Museum Management and Curatorship* 25: 13–35.

Mason, R., Whitehead, C., & Graham, H. (2013). "One Voice to Many Voices? Displaying Polyvocality in an Art Gallery," in *Museums and Communities: Curators, Collections, and Collaboration* (edited by V. Golding & W. Modest). London: Bloomsbury.

Portland Indian Leaders Roundtable. (2007). *Making the Invisible Visible: Portland's Native American Community*. Portland, OR: Portland Indian Leaders Roundtable.

Wood, E., & Latham, K. (2014). *The Objects of Experience: Transforming Visitor-Object Encounters in Museums*. Walnut Creek, CA: Left Coast Press.

Notes

1. Laura Peers, *Playing Ourselves: Interpreting Native Histories at Historic Reconstructions* (Lanham, MD: AltaMira Press, 2007), xxxi.
2. Amy Lonetree, *Decolonizing Museums: Representing Native America in National and Tribal Museums* (Chapel Hill: University of North Carolina Press, 2012), 152.

3. Peers, *Playing Ourselves*, 58.
4. Peers, *Playing Ourselves*, 38.
5. Peers, *Playing Ourselves*, 66.
6. Peers, *Playing Ourselves*, 50.
7. David Hurst Thomas, *Skull Wars: Kennewick Man, Archaeology, and the Battle for Native American Identity* (New York: Basic Books, 2000), 257.
8. Lonetree, *Decolonizing Museums*, 153.
9. Peers, *Playing Ourselves*, 108.
10. Peers, *Playing Ourselves*, 36.
11. Peers, *Playing Ourselves*, 79.
12. Lonetree, *Decolonizing Museums*, 8.
13. Peers, *Playing Ourselves*, 43.
14. Peers, *Playing Ourselves*, 104.
15. Lonetree, *Decolonizing Museums*, 9.
16. Stephen Weil, *Making Museums Matter* (Washington, DC: Smithsonian Institution Press, 2002), 68.
17. James Clifford, "Museums as Contact Zones," in *Routes: Travel and Translation in the Late Twentieth Century*, edited by J. Clifford (Cambridge: Harvard University Press, 1997).
18. Dartt-Newton, "Negotiating the Master Narrative."
19. E. Wood, & K. Latham, *The Objects of Experience: Transforming Visitor-Object Encounters in Museums* (Walnut Creek, CA: Left Coast Press, 2014).
20. M. Hutchison, & L. Collins, "Translations: Experiments in Dialogic Representation of Cultural Diversity in Three Museum Sound Installations." *Museums and Society* 7, no. 2 (2009): 92–109.
21. Portland Indian Leaders Roundtable, *Making the Invisible Visible: Portland's Native American Community* (Portland, OR: Portland Indian Leaders Roundtable, 2007).
22. Dartt-Newton, "Negotiating the Master Narrative."
23. V. Golding, *Learning at the Museum Frontiers: Identity, Race, and Power* (Surrey: Ashgate, 2009); James, "Museums as Contact Zones"; and V. Golding, "Collaborative Museums: Curators, Communities, Collections," in *Museums and Communities: Curators, Collections, and Collaboration*, edited by V. Golding & W. Modest (London: Bloomsbury), 2013.

CHAPTER 7

Pulling It All Together

Native Advisory Councils and Governance

> Traditional wisdom holds that an organization can never change just one thing. So finely balanced are most organizations that change to any one element will ultimately require compensating and sometimes wholly unanticipated changes to many others.[1]

Native Advisory Councils

Thus far, we have introduced ideas about how to begin, build, or improve collaborative relationships with Native American communities, primarily through partnerships based on specific projects, such as exhibits and public programs. Collaborations with Native people for interpreting and accessing collections and developing new school education programs can build on relationships created though project collaborations that are then maintained after the completion of the project. Developing and maintaining relationships takes work, and museum staff should be prepared to make this an ongoing process. When starting a new exhibit project, the curator of the Glenbow Museum in Canada "emphasized the importance of working with a community where contacts have already been made . . . 'if you're going to do something collaboratively, you have to have that relationship, and it takes years to develop.'"[2] Many of the suggestions and examples cited in this book include advisory councils or committees comprised of Native people, which formalizes the relationship between the museum and Native communities and ensures that relationships are not dependent on specific people.

Organizations outside of the museum profession have also created Native advisory councils, including universities, police departments, and nonprofits. There may be a council already established in your area to refer to as an example and to talk to as a resource. Councils are formed in different ways, but out of respect for tribal sovereignty, museum staff should make initial contact with tribal governments, asking if the tribe already has an established method for recommending members to advisory groups. If appropriate, a tribal member might serve as an ambassador, helping to identify the right people to talk to, explaining the process, or speaking to the tribe on behalf of the museum. Either a letter outlining the purpose, time commitments, and compensation for advisory council members can be sent to the head elected tribal official, or making an appointment to speak to him or her, the tribal council, or other appropriate contact can start this process. If the tribe has a process in place for assigning tribal members to councils, be sure to follow that protocol.

Some degree of compensation is appropriate because members of the council are giving their time and expertise. If council members are required to travel to meetings, reimbursement for mileage, hotel, and food should be included in the budget. Annual (or more frequent as needed) meetings at the museum can bring everyone together to learn more about the activities of the museum and to focus the purpose of the meeting on museum programs, exhibits, governance, interpretation, or other pressing issues. Some advisory councils also meet periodically on tribal lands. There are many benefits of meeting in a tribal community—some of which have already been outlined—such as learning more about the issues important to the tribe and meeting community members who might not travel to the museum. It also gives the tribe an opportunity to host a meeting in a forum that reflects their cultural values, something that is less likely to happen at the museum. Meeting on tribal territory reinforces the goals of authority sharing and can help ensure all members of the advisory group are open to different ideas and ways of thinking.

Structure the meeting in such a way that there is time for sharing and questions-and-answers from all parties. There should be an agenda set in advance and sent to everyone outlining the goals for the meeting. If possible, have the meeting catered; this will respect personal needs and reduce the need for people to come and go, allowing members of the council to focus on the purpose of the meeting.

Advisory groups have many functions: they can focus exclusively on exhibits, to help develop themes, objects, images, content, and edit the final exhibit script. "What drove the content decisions for the new museum were not objects but concepts. The advisory board (at Mille Lacs) put forward ideas that focused on contemporary life. From day one . . . the Band's sovereign status was central to the new museum."[3] These groups can also go further, to offer advice about how Native American history and culture is represented to the public, collecting goals, policies, and practices, the museum shop, and overall governance. The point is to be "transparent in [the] decision making and willing to share power. New museum theory is about decolonizing, giving those represented control over their own cultural heritage."[4]

How It All Comes Together

With an advisory council in place, and open communication between museum staff and Native stakeholders, pulling it all together becomes possible. Exhibits and the exhibit process have received a lot of attention, and rightfully so, because exhibits are the most common way that visitors interact with a museum. "Ira Jacknis has argued that, in many respects, a museum is 'synonymous with its exhibitions.'" Exhibits are 'a tangible and visible expression of a museum's fundamental concepts and values.'"[5]

Developing an exhibit process that is truly inclusive of Native people and shares authority is an important step in fully representing Native people and communities. "Developing community-collaborative exhibits demands more than just being well versed in the scholarly literature on respective topics or on the latest in exhibition practices. It is about building trust, developing relationships, communicating, sharing authority, and being humble."[6] The lessons learned from exhibit collaborations can be applied more broadly to other collaborations and relationships. Knowing the history and use for objects in the collection from a Native perspective and incorporating this information into collections data respects Native authority, knowledge, and values. To be able to interpret Native American history and culture, it is imperative that Native perspectives and knowledge be valued equally, or preferentially, as other sources of information.

Visitors bring with them knowledge and misconceptions about American history; they already "know" the dominant narrative of western expansion and the formation of the United States. What most visitors have never encountered is alternative versions of this same history—accounts of events, time periods, and people, told from a different, yet equally (or sometimes more) honest perspective. The need to present a "balanced" interpretation is diminished in light of this fact. Interpretation of Native history can focus less on retelling old, tired stories, and allow for fresh perspectives that challenge visitor assumptions. Visitors come to museums expecting to learn something new, which gives museum interpreters the opportunity to embrace that responsibility and provide a platform for Native voice and perspective that engages with people in new ways.

Beyond Exhibits and Programs

Interpretation does not stop when visitors leave an exhibit or program; it takes place in all museum spaces. Front-line staff must be trained to recognize their own bias or ignorance about Native issues and to prevent personal opinions from influencing visitor experience. Front-line staffs also need to be prepared to address visitor comments that represent stereotypes, racism, or ignorance. During staff and volunteer orientation the stereotyping activity in appendix 2 can be used as an exercise in identifying stereotypes about Native people or culture to understand where they come from. *Do All Indians Live in Tipis* by the National Museum of the American Indian is a great resource to help answer visitor questions. The book answers some of the most commonly asked questions about Native people, in short, simple answers.

The museum shop is also an extension of interpretation. If there are products sold in the shop that include stereotypes of Native people, undermine cultural and religious sovereignty, or are inaccurate, the museum could be seen as endorsing those products. "If visitors 'consume' history and nostalgia . . . , they do so most literally in the shops, and the images they take home with them are crucial to either reinforcing stereotypes, or challenging them."[7]

Think of the implications if educational, public programs, and exhibits address issues related to the importance of modern Native American craft, showcasing the works of local Native artists, yet the shop sells products made overseas or by non-Native people. How will visitors take seriously the concerns of Native people about cultural and religious appropriation if a museum shop sells smudge sticks, feather fans, and how-to books about Native spirituality? Visitors will be getting mixed messages, and the museum shop, as an extension of the museum itself, is considered a trusted source for purchasing products that are responsible. "Pulling it all together" means looking at everything the museum does and taking time to consider the implications, and whether business as usual in one area of the museum could be undermining the hard work and changes made in another.

Visitor Reactions and Feedback

Laura Peers recently conducted a study detailing the opportunities and challenges facing Native interpreters at living history sites. Based on her research, she speculates that there is a "growing popular desire to understand Native people and to include them as members of North American society . . . there is, I think, a growing acceptance of Native cultures as distinct elements of society. . . . Many visitors are fascinated by the Native elements of these sites, and actively construct new meanings."[8]

Research indicates that visitors respond favorably to first-person Native voice as the primary source of information in exhibits and public programs. Visitors in Australia were asked about a new exhibit at the Australian Museum in Sidney that included first-person Native voice that "showed an increase in understanding as well as engendering a sense of empathy for the way Indigenous people had been treated in the past. . . . Crucially, visitors reported that the prominence of the Aboriginal voices in the exhibition, especially the use of first-person quotes, was important in their learning process."[9]

When Native people have control over, or lead the process of telling their own stories, as we have seen, the focus of the stories changes. "Many visitors did recognize and appreciate the contemporary themes presented in the [Mille Lacs] museum. Some visitor responses include 'I was happily surprised at the incorporation of the present day Ojibwe Indians in the exhibit,' and 'Wonderful exhibit. Much respect was used in putting it together. It is an honest representation of native life.'"[10]

There are different measures to determine success in exhibits that feature Native perspective as the primary voice. Non-Native visitors reported feedback to the Utah Museum of Natural History "*Native Voices*" exhibit with comments such as: "Will remember the bear-dancing video in *Native Voices* and that Native Americans are not just a piece of history, but are active in current times in Utah," and "The Native area was very emotional."[11]

For Native visitors, a measure of success can be found in comments that inspire sharing between families and generations, increased pride in Native identity and traditions, and deeper appreciation and understanding of their history and culture. At the Utah Museum of Natural History, a staff member observed an interaction between several children and their grandfather as they watched a video that included traditional dancing. One of the children asked, "Grandpa, can we learn to dance like that?" to which the man replied, "We'll have to have Grandma show you how when we get home."[12] Kelli Mosteller, Director of the Cultural Heritage Center, Citizen Potawatomi, reports that members of another Potawatomi Nation were visiting the Cultural Center:

> I was giving them a tour and as we approached the Seven Fires exhibit, which portrays a story that is part of the Potawatomi oral tradition, all of them immediately knew what it was. It is an exhibit that could easily be mistaken as simply a council fire or some other

> kind of scene by those who don't know the story, but because of their knowledge they recognized all of the finer details that we spent months ensuring we got right. We then started talking about the different ways we had learned the story and how each community of Potawatomi goes about passing it along to the younger generations. It was very rewarding to feel like our work was not only educational to those who are not familiar with the Seven Fires teachings, but a source of inspiration and dialogue for those who grew up with the story and hold it as sacred.[13]

Of course, not everyone appreciates or understands the importance of these changes. Native and non-Native visitors alike have criticized the move to tell Native history through Native voice and to incorporate contemporary issues and communities in Native exhibits. There have been many articles and books written about the National Museum of the American Indian that criticize the structure and content of the exhibits.

The Utah Museum of Natural History also reported visitor feedback and reviews of the "*Native Voices*" exhibit that demonstrated lack of appreciation or understanding of the importance of authority sharing. Becky Menlove shared, "*The New York Times* review of our '*Native Voices*' exhibit referred to the content as something like "platitudes we've all heard before," which to my mind revealed lack of understanding by the writer about the Utah tribes whose representatives so wanted to reveal a history that is little known."[14]

Native people may also criticize exhibits that share authority or rely on first-person voice as sharing too much with non-Natives, telling painful stories that are best left to the past, or using language that could be interpreted as Native people being victims or passive. All critiques—positive or negative—are important tools for learning and improving the process moving forward and should not be interpreted as failure. Staff and museum leadership should not be discouraged from this work by negative feedback, but should use that feedback to build stronger partnerships in the future and to inspire new ideas for future topics.

> Moving to a place of respect and privileging Native voice in museum work inevitably involves painful experiences. These experiences need not be a cause for negative judgments or taking things personally. Rather, they show that participants are engaged in an authentic, transformative process. As with any relationship, the challenge lies in how we respond to these experiences when they arise.[15]

The Impact of Working Inclusively

Museums as places of collecting, preserving, learning, and as a profession have changed dramatically over the past century. After World War I, museums "took as its basic tasks to gather, preserve, and study the record of human and natural history. Any further benefit, such as providing the public with physical and intellectual access to the collections and information thus accumulated, was simply a plus. Fifty years later, caught up in the confluence of two powerful currents . . . the American museum is being substantially reshaped."[16] Community and education are now as central to the mission of museums as collecting and preserving, and many are focused on social issues and as serving as community forums to help solve problems. Harold Skramstad, president emeritus of the Henry Ford, pointed out that "unless museums can and do play a role relative to the real problems of real people's lives, then what is their point?"[17] Stephen Weil goes on to ask, "If our museums are *not* being operated with the ultimate goal of improving the quality of people's lives, on what [other] basis might we possibly ask for public support?"[18] Museums that collect and interpret Native history and culture have the potential to help rewrite popular misconceptions of history, by working in partnership with Native communities who are expert in knowing and sharing stories about events, people, and cultures that history books often leave out. Native advisory councils, Native interpreters, educators, and staff, have the ability to foster deeper, lasting understandings than non-Native interpreters telling Native history in the third person. "Beyond their capacity to enrich already existing relationships, museums might also contribute to the creation of important new relationships."[19]

Peers calls the encounters between Native presenters and interpreters and white visitors at historic sites and museums "contact zones." "In these places, people of different backgrounds meet: for visitors who have never met a Native person before, these are first encounters. And although visitors to historic sites often draw on stereotyped images of Native people in their responses to Native interpreters, these are also places where such assumptions are challenged and revised."[20] In its strategic agenda for 1998–2000, American Alliance of Museums (AAM) referred to museums as institutions that can help build community. "In that view, the museum may be considered as a distinctive public space, in which diverse elements of the community might intermingle in ways not readily available elsewhere. . . . Elaine Heumann Gurian has argued that—because of the high degree of public trust they enjoy—museums should also be recognized as one of the few institutions within a community that can function as a safety zone . . . in which members of a minority group might hope to socialize without fear of intimidation."[21]

Strong, institution-wide commitment to involve Native advisors is a slow and steady process that needs to be adopted by the leadership of the museum as a priority, and implemented in staff and board orientation and training. Institution-wide buy-in is important to ensure that changes in staff and leadership do not change the commitment to inclusive Native representation in museum practices. "Nina Archabal [Deputy Director of the Mille Lacs Indian Museum] said 'I would say that ten or fifteen years of good work on the part of the staff members here and good heart does not take away years and years and decades and decades of distrust.' It simply indicates that asserting Native voice and decolonizing are processes: they involve many steps and stages."[22]

Conclusion: Decolonizing

The word *decolonizing* has been mentioned several times in this book, but what does it mean? There are, of course, different opinions about what it means to decolonize a museum, and if it is even the right word, or possible at all. To understand what it means to decolonize, it is helpful to know what colonization means. *Colonize* can be defined as "To resettle or confine (persons) in or as if in a colony. To subjugate (a population) to or as if to a colonial government."[23] To *decolonize* can be defined as "to free a colony to become self-governing or independent."[24] If we take the spirit of the two definitions and apply them to the complex history between museums and Native communities, it is clear that museums have a history of subjugating the understanding of Native sovereignty, culture, and people by leaving Native people out of the process and retelling stories of dominance that justified colonization. Therefore, to decolonize, museums must free Native people to become independent of this process and enable them to tell their own stories. Amy Lonetree has literally written the book on decolonizing museums, and she points out that "decolonizing museum practice must involve assisting our communities in addressing the legacies of historical unresolved grief."[25] To decolonize becomes more than creating space and authority for Native people to advise museum practice and content, but rather to actively engage all museum activities in seeking to address hard truths and heal past wrongs. At the time that the National Museum of the American Indian was being created, then Smithsonian Secretary Robert McAdams said of that institution, "It envisions a partnership of a new and unprecedented kind—with those whose history and culture, once torn away from them, will now be represented only with their full complicity."[26]

If we are to consider best practices for interpreting Native American history and culture in museums, we must realize that it goes beyond telling contemporary stories, beyond creating a venue for direct Native voice, and envisions a future in which museums and Native people work together to create a more inclusive and informed society. "As we look to the future, I believe it is critical that museums support Indigenous communities in our efforts toward decolonization. This includes a commitment on the part of museums to privilege Indigenous voices and perspectives, to challenge stereotypical representations of Native people that were produced in the past, and to serve as educational forums for our own communities and the public. Furthermore, the hard truths of our history need to be stated to a nation that has willfully sought to silence our version of the past."[27]

These relationships and commitments on the parts of both museums and Native communities will result in institutions that realize the potential that Skramstad and Weil challenge modern museums to embrace, one of meaning, where community problems are addressed, and the museum becomes a resource for strengthening community relations and solving real problems for real people. What does that look like for museums that work to decolonize in partnership with Native people?

> What happens when museums do decolonizing work? Museums become places for building momentum for healing, for community, and for restoring dignity and respect. By using the focus of Indigenous peoples to guide their work, those involved in developing museums change what museums are all about. Museums cease to function as places of oppression or for perpetrating colonizer-serving images and models. The decolonizing direction enables museums to become places for decolonizing the representations of Native peoples and for promoting community healing and empowerment.[28]

CASE STUDY: COLLABORATING WITH CULTURES: THE EITELJORG

MUSEUM OF AMERICAN INDIANS AND WESTERN ART

James H. Nottage, Vice President, Eiteljorg Museum

The President and CEO of the Eiteljorg Museum, John Vanausdall, says it all in a direct and meaningful statement: "you cannot be a museum 'about' Native Americans unless you are 'with' Native Americans." This institution has been willing to share authority with Native peoples from its founding, and has become more skilled at doing so through time. Success can be measured by the engagement of Native Americans on the board, staff, as members, artists, advisors, and as cultural representatives, not just as subjects, but as part of the very fabric of the museum.

In 2014, the Eiteljorg celebrated twenty-five years since first opening its imposing mahogany doors to a public that now totals more than two million visitors annually. During those years, the institution's public spaces have doubled in size, collections have expanded by three times, and programs have connected with audiences of all ages. The museum has produced a broad range of exhibitions, publications, and educational tools and experiences. Along the way, it has grown from childhood to become a young adult; it is now experienced, wiser, and motivated to continue along a path consistently marked by devotion to mission and providing forums for sharing its voice with the subjects it interprets. In truth, many voices of staff, board, members, donors, artists, and cultural representatives have combined to shape the institution. Following is a summary of those voices and their engagement within the museum.

Origins of the Eiteljorg Museum can be found in the passions and dedication of two Indianapolis collectors. Harrison Eiteljorg, a successful businessman involved in mining, had the means to collect in a number of areas. As a community leader, he served as board chair for the Indianapolis Museum of Art, where his vast holdings in African art became the basis of their notable collection in that field. His passions for art of the American West and for Native American cultural objects were the focal points not just for collecting, but also for encouraging the work of living artists. The breadth of his holdings embraced traditional realist art of the West by painters and sculptors such as Frederic Remington, Henry Farny, and Albert Bierstadt. He also gravitated toward early modernists active in Taos and Santa Fe, New Mexico, such as Marsden Hartley, John Sloan, Robert Henri, and Georgia O'Keeffe. This ultimately informed his efforts in the 1960s through 1980s to collect important works by Native painters such as Fritz Scholder and T. C. Cannon. Eiteljorg's collection of Native objects such as pottery, baskets, clothing, masks, weapons, and weavings was just as aggressively formed.[29]

James Lawton, an equally devoted collector with a focus on all things Native American, had developed a private museum at the former summer home of J. K. Lilly in Eagle Creek Park. Founded in 1967, his museum and the collection served a generation of school children, but by the 1980s, Lawton's museum faced the possibility of closing, until a set of circumstances came together.[30]

With visionary leadership and economic growth, Indianapolis's "public, business, and philanthropic" interests joined to develop a master plan for an urban park and a cultural district. Downtown would undergo a renaissance, including development of White River State Park. In the 1980s, city efforts to acquire the famed but foundering Museum of the American Indian, Heye Foundation, of New York City, came to naught as legal action and national legislation saw to the eventual formation of the Smithsonian's National Museum of the American Indian. Soon, another opportunity came to be a reality. As a key part of park development, Harrison Eiteljorg agreed to donate his collection to a new nonprofit museum; it would absorb Lawton's museum to form the Eiteljorg Museum of American Indian and Western Art.

The institution was originally conceived of as an art museum and initial core exhibit galleries were planned with ideas expressed by curator Mike Leslie who wrote that:

> to appreciate American Indian art, one must more fully understand their culture, their environment, and their history. . . . The museum's overall programming emphasizes not only the historical importance of Native American art and artifacts, but also their importance in a modern context. We must not forget that Native American cultures are still flourishing artistically.

The approach taken was to arrange objects in sections based on culture group concepts to "provide the visitor with a broad understanding of Native American culture within an anthropological, geographical, and historical context."[31]

The history of the museum's earliest work with Native American advisors is not thoroughly documented, but it is clear that academic and curatorial expertise was supplemented through such consultation. In June 1989, the Eiteljorg opened to enthusiastic audiences and the community celebrated. Although the museum administrators also celebrated an opening that came off "without a hitch," not all Native communities were as satisfied. "A moving invocation by Wap-Shing of the Miami Tribe" was part of the celebration, but lengthy proceedings that followed introduced representatives of Blackfeet and other tribes from further West. The museum felt it was doing the right things, but it did not understand how members of the Miami Nation of Indiana reacted. They felt a sense of exclusion that would simmer for the next three years.[32]

The Eiteljorg began producing and hosting significant exhibitions on Native American subjects. *Crossroads of Continents*, a joint project of Smithsonian and Russian curators, was featured in 1990, making it necessary to dismantle core exhibits, which were reinstalled the next year. During this time, the Eiteljorg formed its Native American National Advisory Council, which contributed to development of the spaces. Hopi and Winnebago/Sioux members attended the opening dedication in the spring of 1991. Other members of the council included artists and cultural representatives from the Potawatomi, Tlingit, and Blackfeet tribes.[33]

Institutional satisfaction at having such a learned group contributing to the work of the staff was not enough—something that would soon be acknowledged. The perspective and frustrations of the Miami Nation of Indiana came through a letter from an intermediary. The

Eiteljorg director, Michael Duty, responded to the letter, acknowledging that the museum worked hard to involve Native Americans in programs and exhibitions, and the perception of the Miami was taken seriously. Being in the homeland of the Miami, the museum needed to be more engaged with them and to more effectively acknowledge how important they were as a continuing part of life in Indiana.[34] The next several years would be pivotal in the development of new relationships with the Miami and other Native peoples. The museum board, staff, and advisory group would mature significantly over the next five years.

In the summer of 1992, the American Indian Advisory council met formally, evaluating exhibitions, collections policies and priorities, and past programming. New members included individuals from the Eastern Band of Cherokee, the Maricopa, and Navajo. A board liaison was appointed to facilitate communications. Most importantly the group worked to define itself, determining the frequency of meetings, the need to work directly with the Miami chief, and writing a council mission statement with the following description:

> The American Indian Advisory Board (AIAB) shall work directly with the museum's Board of Directors, the Executive Director, the Chief Curator, and the Associate Curator for Ethnology in providing guidance, assistance and direction in all matters associated with the art, culture, and history of native peoples of North America. The American Indian Advisory Board shall provide instruction to the Collections Council and the Education and Exhibition Council on issues relating to the acquisition of Native American art, the repatriation of cultural property, the display and interpretation of art, and the development of related public programming. In addition, the AIAB shall respond to Native American community issues and oversee the establishment and implementation of guidelines concerning cultural sensitivity.

Policies were generated by the group to guide the museum in matters such as confirming that demonstrators and artists featured at the museum were, indeed, enrolled tribal members. Plans were shared and developed further on the matter of creating an annual Indian Market, with council members taking on the role of jurors for the market. Consideration was also given to how the museum should manage potentially sacred objects and related records and images of the objects. One clear message was that the museum needed to consider the differences between ownership and stewardship related to sacred or sensitive objects. This meeting and the next helped to confirm and define a clear path for the museum to conform to the reporting requirements of the Native American Graves Protection and Repatriation Act (NAGPRA). The council would work with the museum as it responded to the law and delivered summaries of unassociated funerary objects, sacred objects, and objects of cultural patrimony to the tribes by November 16, 1993.[35]

Work with Indiana Miami Chief, Raymond White, confirmed the appointment of Carl T. Lavoncher II to the council. Representation on the council was now both national and regional. Further, by the middle 1990s two especially significant Miami became more deeply engaged, serving as members of the board of directors, providing wise counsel and becoming close friends of the institution. Miami Nation elder, Lora Siders, became a member of the board of directors that also included Henry Bush, Jr., of the Potawatomi. With the passing of Siders, Vice Chief of the Miami Nation of Indiana, Frances Dunnagan, became a board member.[36] Significantly, Dunnagan and Bush were on the search committee for a new museum CEO when Vanausdall was hired in 1997. Relationships between the museum and Native peoples by the last half of the 1990s were no longer a matter of something that should be, but a mutually embraced set of relationships that all parties supported and benefited from.

It was a pivotal event in the fall of 1997 that most clearly demonstrated the depth of new relationships. Vanausdall described the exhibition, *In the Presence of the Past: The Miami Indians of Indiana*, as "a new level of community partnership." It was the first national exhibition to examine the Miami story and it grew out of working directly with the Miami tribal council in Peru, Indiana, and explored "with them the contributions our Native American hosts have made to the history of this region." Gathering major objects from museum and private collections throughout the country, the show was presented as an "exciting living history context for the works of art being shown. Landscape, architecture, stories and interviews, clothing, diplomatic gifts, trade goods, documents and photographs, music and narrative sound . . . [were] woven together to give a vital picture of the Miami during the last two centuries." Meaningfully, the show confirmed the vitality of the Miami as a living part of Indiana life to the present day. "The museum assembled a seven-member Miami Indian Advisory Panel to help guide the exhibit." At the conclusion of the show, the exhibition panels were given to the Miami of Indiana for use in their offices in Peru, Indiana. Readers of this narrative should note that the Indiana Miami are not recognized by the state or federal governments. The staff also developed relationships with the federally recognized Miami of Oklahoma.[37]

Two years prior to the opening of the Miami exhibition, another highly significant event took place. In August 1995, it was announced that a new staff position had been made possible through a grant from the Indianapolis Foundation. The curator of Native American art and culture would be charged not only with responsibility for the Miami exhibition but with upgrading all the second-floor exhibitions in the museum. The museum newsletter announcing this development, also celebrated the hiring of Ray Gonyea to fill the position. A member of the beaver clan of the Onondaga tribe of the Iroquois nation, Gonyea was recruited from the National Museum of the American Indian. He was a pioneering curator among Native Americans and brought new respect to the institution.[38]

Redevelopment of the Native American galleries would also require a reinvigoration of the council. Toward that end, chief curatorial officer Arnold Jolles invited council member, R. David Edmunds (Eastern Band of Cherokee) to serve in a leadership position for the council. As a distinguished author and professor, Edmunds had taught at the University of Indiana and then moved to the University of Texas at Dallas. Edmunds accepted the invitation and one year later, the renamed Native American Council adopted a new mission statement:

> The Native American Council shall work directly with the President and CEO, and with the Vice president, Curator of Native American Art and Culture, other councils and members of the board and staff as required, to provide information and counsel regarding Native American art, history and culture as presented in the museum's exhibitions, programs, publications and collections. It will also serve as a source of information to the nation's Native American communities regarding the activities of the Eiteljorg Museum.

The officially adopted objectives of the council would see it functioning as:

> a vital source of information, expertise, and cultural contacts. These will be used to help develop the museum's collecting policies, to enrich the reinstallation of the museum's Native American collections, and to suggest topics for special exhibitions, research and publication. Council members are selected to represent a broad cross section of cultures, geographical areas, types of expertise, and experience. With the help of the Council the Eiteljorg Museum hopes to make Indianapolis an important Midwestern destination for informal learning and a site where our school communities, families, and lifelong learners can encounter and enjoy the richness of Native American cultures and history.[39]

The museum staff team and National Advisory Council immediately focused on the momentum built from the Miami exhibition. The new council met for the first time on March 6, 1998. Discussions focused on reinstallation of the gallery and the interpretive themes to be considered. Under the leadership of Edmunds, changes to the council had brought other leading scholars and cultural representatives to the group including: Dr. Donald Fixico (Shawnee/Sac and Fox/Muscogee Creek/Seminole) then at the University of Kansas; Dr. Brenda Child (Ojibwe) at the University of Minnesota; architect Dennis Sun Rhodes (Arapaho) from St. Paul; Gloria Lomahaftewa (Hopi/Choctaw); Dr. James Riding In (Pawnee) from Arizona State University; Juanita G. Corbine Espinosa (Dakota/Ojibway), director of Native Arts Circle, Minnesota's first statewide Native American arts agency; Richard W. Hill, Sr. (Tuscarora Nation); and John Murray (Blackfeet).

Combined with staff curators, an exhibition developer, designer, collection specialists, educators, and administrators, the overall efforts were to explore alternatives to presenting the stories of Native Americans within the interpretive limits of simply dividing the galleries into culture groups. Interpretive ideas related to ecology, history and cultural practices, migration, trade, technology, and other themes were explored, and a number of critical conclusions were arrived at. An overriding object would be for the Eiteljorg to "become an unavoidable resource for regional school systems." It would "create a singularly exciting presentation of the cultures of indigenous North American peoples" and "use cooperative advisory networks, exhibitions, publications, electronic/media communications, and cooperative interagency programming where families, lifelong learners and tourists, can find an engaging presentation of Native American cultures past and present." The museum would display and interpret its most important Native American holdings and bring significant borrowed Native American resources to Indianapolis. Above all, it would follow sound conservation practice along with sound Native American cultural practices.[40]

By November 1999, the council and staff agreed that the initial focus would be on the interpretation of the Native peoples of Indiana, giving them a permanent place in the galleries. To develop this first part of the galleries the council advised how important it would be to appoint a special "Native American Regional Advisory Group." It was not long before the museum publicly announced that such a group had been formed to "provide guidance to museum staff working on Native American exhibitions, events and issues." With the support of Miami Chief Paul Strack, Chief of the Delaware, Dee Ketchum, and the cultural committee of the Pokagon Potawatomi, the following individuals accepted appointments to the special council: Daryl Baldwin (Miami Nation), John Warren (Potawatomi, Pokagon band), and Don Secondine (Delaware). They would begin working with staff by focusing upon three concepts: the richness of human experience, relationships, and creativity; conveying information in Native American "voice," philosophy and practice; and concentrate on the Miami Indians and their close Central Algonquian neighbors."[41] With the regional council's input, other members of these groups became engaged as informants and as artists included in the exhibit. One of these, Scott Shoemaker of the Miami Nation of Indiana, later became a member of the National Advisory Council and continues to inform, inspire, and collaborate in the ongoing work of the museum.

By January 2001, a focused concept for the new gallery had been determined: "Through Native American Woodlands objects, historical and cultural information and multimedia, this exhibition/installation will provide awareness of the art, history, cultural and contemporary issues of woodland cultures/communities—especially those communities specific to this region." Overarching themes would be the people, trade and exchange, and adoption and adaptation. To express these, specific goals and objectives for the space were also defined.

Resulting from close collaboration with both the national and regional councils, the engaging exhibition with main panels written by the representatives from the Miami, Potawatomi, and Delaware tribes opened in summer 2002 (Figure 7.1). Titled "*Mihtohseenionki* (The People's Place)," the gallery included important loans from Chicago, Detroit, Washington, and elsewhere. In 2002, the Eiteljorg formed a unique partnership with the Smithsonian National Museum of the American Indian (NMAI) that allowed the institution to borrow

Figure 7.1. Members of the Miami Tribe of Indiana tour *Mihtohseenionki* for the first time in 2002. *Source:* Eiteljorg Museum of American Indians and Western Art, Indianapolis, IN

deeply from the collections of the NMAI, making it possible to significantly enrich the galleries. Interactive terminals won a gold medal from the American Alliance of Museums (AAM). A printed 140-page resource guide for Indiana K–12 provided materials for teachers focused on the Miami story and was distributed free of charge and also made available on the institution's website.

Most significantly, the show was first opened to members of the Miami, Potawatomi, and Delaware tribes (Figure 7.2). A year before the opening Chief Paul Strack of the Miami of Indiana, on behalf of the cultural committee of the tribe, presented a check to museum CEO Vanausdall to contribute toward the institution's expansion campaign. At the opening, Chief Strack, speaking for the museum's board of directors, welcomed Indiana and Oklahoma Miami, Delaware, and Pokagon Potawatomi representatives. Chiefs for all the tribes, their respective council representatives, and many family members were all in attendance. For some, the gathering was the first time families had connected with each other in a long time. For many, the exhibit was highly personal.[42]

Miami artist Dani Tippmann later wrote a thank you note, stating that "I cannot tell you how moving seeing the new permanent exhibit last night was for me. As I entered the *Mihtohseenionki* on my right was an image of my grandfather on the screen as a part of the movie. I went a little farther and on the left an image of my daughter on the interactive map caught my eye. Those first few moments summed up the exhibit. You have honored the past and the future by creating *Mihtohseenionki* for the people of today."[43]

Figure 7.2. Ribbon-cutting ceremony for "Mihtohseenionki (The People's Place)", 2002. Left to right: Brian Buchanan, Chief Miami Tribe of Indiana; Julie Olds, Miami Tribe of Oklahoma; John Vanausdall, President and CEO Eiteljorg Museum; Don Secondine, Delaware Tribe of Oklahoma. *Source:* Eiteljorg Museum of American Indians and Western Art, Indianapolis, IN

The Eiteljorg Museum of American Indians and Western art continues to nurture its many different relationships with Native Americans (Figure 7.3). The national and regional advisors continue working to inform the institution's efforts even though it is important at this point in time to reinvigorate activities of the councils. Reinstallation of the Native American galleries is not complete. Priority as of this writing is being given to making our activities sustainable. Endowment funds to support the position and work of the curator of Native American art, history, and culture are being developed. Collections are growing with contributions from a number of leading collectors. Public programs have become more dynamic by inclusion of an interactive family gallery and the provision of an artist-in-residence program that brings many traditional artists to the museum and to area school systems.[44]

One change to the national council over the last several years has been the addition of Native American contemporary artists and art scholars. In 1999, the Eiteljorg launched the Eiteljorg Contemporary Art Fellowship. This biennial project honors a distinguished artist and four other fellows with an exhibition, book, symposia, and the addition of their work to the museum collection. Each artist also receives a $25,000 fellowship award. This singular

Figure 7.3. Representatives of the Miami, Delaware, Potawatomi, and other tribes participating in opening ceremony for the Eiteljorg Museum expansion in 2005. *Source:* Eiteljorg Museum of American Indians and Western Art, Indianapolis, IN

program has made the Eiteljorg the leading influence in contemporary Native American art, making the institution a center for scholarship and understanding for the field. Selectors for the show, authors for the publication, and presenters at the symposia are drawn from leading curators, professors, and commentators in the field and as frequently as possible they are Native American.[45]

What conclusions might you draw from this narrative of the Eiteljorg experience about working with Native Americans? Have we done everything right, or have we effectively learned from our experiences? We know that even with the best of intentions we have made errors, but we have always been committed to learning from our experiences and moving forward. The reason we have succeeded is that at all levels Native Americans are engaged with the museum. There are important individuals on the board of directors, on the staff, on advisory councils, among our artists and visitors and as donors to the museum. We want and need more active participation, but the point is that there is not a clear separation between the museum and Native Americans.

The museum has been fortunate to benefit from significant financial support from individuals and foundations for some of our programs, but things we have done can be accomplished on the most slender of budgets at any museum. It is not the size of your budget that counts. It is the size of your commitment to sharing authority, welcoming and engaging with the communities, and being relevant to all of your present and future audiences. It should go without saying that this is not about being politically correct. It is about creating the best products possible, about being inclusive of your audiences, and about providing the public with understanding and appreciation for the fact that just like you, Native Americans are about the past and the present and that they have much to share about themselves.

Notes

1. Stephen Weil, *Making Museums Matter* (Washington, DC: Smithsonian Institution Press, 2002), 41.
2. Amy Lonetree, *Decolonizing Museums: Representing Native America in National and Tribal Museums* (Chapel Hill: University of North Carolina Press, 2012), 42–43.
3. Lonetree, *Decolonizing Museums*, 46.
4. Lonetree, *Decolonizing Museums*, 172.
5. Lonetree, *Decolonizing Museums*, 107.
6. Lonetree, *Decolonizing Museums*, 170.
7. Laura Peers, *Playing Ourselves: Interpreting Native Histories at Historic Reconstructions* (Lanham, MD: AltaMira Press, 2007), 128.
8. Peers, *Playing Ourselves*, 137.
9. Peers, *Playing Ourselves*, 152.
10. Lonetree, *Decolonizing Museums*, 65.
11. Becky Menlove, personal communication, January 11, 2014.
12. Becky Menlove, personal communication, January 11, 2014.
13. Kelli Mosteller, personal communication, January 11, 2014.
14. Becky Menlove, personal communication, January 11, 2014.
15. Lonetree, *Decolonizing Museums*, 107.

16. Weil, *Making Museums Matter*, 28.
17. Weil, *Making Museums Matter*, 39.
18. Weil, *Making Museums Matter*, 39.
19. Weil, *Making Museums Matter*, 67.
20. Peers, *Playing Ourselves*, 143.
21. Weil, *Making Museums Matter*, 68.
22. Lonetree, *Decolonizing Museums*, 69.
23. Yahoo online dictionary, "colonize," http://dictionary.search.yahoo.com/search;_ylt=A0oG7lcffdFS3lAAiRtXNyoA;_ylu=X3oDMTBzdWdjNGdsBHNlYwNzYwRjb2xvA2FjMgR2dGlkA1FJMDQ5XzE-?p=colonize, accessed January 11, 2014.
24. Dictionary.com, "decolonize," http://dictionary.reference.com/browse/decolonize, accessed January 11, 2014.
25. Lonetree, *Decolonizing Museums*, 5.
26. Patricia Pierce Erikson, "Decolonizing the 'Nation's Attic,'" in *The National Museum of the American Indian: Critical Conversations*, edited by Amy Lonetree and Amanda J. Cobb (Lincoln: University of Nebraska Press, 2008), 48.
27. Lonetree, *Decolonizing Museums*, 166.
28. Lonetree, *Decolonizing Museums*, 171.
29. Theodore Celenko, *A Treasury of African Art from the Harrison Eiteljorg Collection* (Bloomington: Indiana University Press, 1984). Harrison Eiteljorg, *Treasures of the American West, Selections from the Collection of Harrison Eiteljorg*, foreword by Patricia Janis Broder (New York: Balance House, 1981).
30. For a general history of the Eiteljorg Museum, see *Frontiers and Beyond, Visions and Collections from the Eiteljorg Museum of American Indians and Western Art* (Indianapolis: Eiteljorg Museum of American Indians and Western Art, 2005). Specifically see, John Vanausdall, "The Museum Grows Up," and Jeanette Vanausdall, "Harrison Eiteljorg, Museum Founder." See also, Eiteljorg Museum of American Indian and Western Art, *Newsletter*, January/February 1989, page 1.
31. Eiteljorg Museum of American Indian and Western Art, *Newsletter*, November/December 1988.
32. Eiteljorg Museum of American Indian and Western Art *Newsletter*, July/August 1989; Eiteljorg Museum of American Indian and Western Art *Newsletter*, Fall 1989.
33. Eiteljorg Museum of American Indian and Western Art *Newsletter*, summer 1990; Eiteljorg Museum of American Indian and Western Art *Newsletter*, fall 1990; Eiteljorg Museum of American Indian and Western Art *Newsletter*, spring, 1991.
34. Letter Sent, Nick Clark to Michael Duty, June 8, 1992; Duty to Clark, June 19, 1992; institutional archives, Eiteljorg Museum.
35. Eiteljorg Museum of American Indian and Western Art *Newsletter*, summer 1992; American Indian Advisory Council meeting minutes, May 5–7, 1992, and September 24, 1993; Eiteljorg Museum of American Indian and Western Art *Newsletter*, spring 1993; Eiteljorg Museum of American Indian and Western Art *Newsletter*, summer 1995.
36. In 2013, Frances Dunnagan's granddaughter, Erin Oliver, became a board member, continuing her family's ties to the Eiteljorg and its mission.
37. Eiteljorg Museum of American Indian and Western Art *Newsletter*, January 1997; Eiteljorg Museum of American Indian and Western Art *Newsletter*, April 1997; Eiteljorg Museum of American Indian and Western Art *Newsletter*, first quarter 1999; Eiteljorg Museum of American Indian and Western Art *Newsletter*, first quarter 2001.

38. Eiteljorg Museum of American Indian and Western Art *Newsletter*, August 1995.
39. LS Arnold Jolles to R. David Edmunds, June 27, 1997; Memo; Arnold Jolles, regarding council, February 24, 1998; National Advisory Council, meeting minutes, March 6–7, 1998. Native American Council, mission statement, April 2, 1998.
40. Native American Council meeting minutes, March 6, 1998.
41. National Native American Council, meeting minutes, November 14, 1999, and March 12, 2000; Eiteljorg Museum of American Indian and Western Art *Newsletter*, 4th quarter 2000.
42. NA Reinstallation team meeting minutes, January 5, 2001. Eiteljorg Museum of American Indian and Western Art *Newsletter*, spring/summer, 2002; page 3, "*Mihtohseenionki* (The People's Place)." Much of the gallery's success is owed to exhibition developer Tricia O'Connor, director of exhibition design Steve Sipe, and curator of Native American art, history and culture, Ray Gonyea. Letter Sent, Paul L. Strack to John Vanausdall, October 12, 2001. Script, opening remarks for *Mihtohseenionki*, June 12, 2002. Invitation, for eagle society and donor preview of *Mihtohseenionki* ("The People's Place"), June 12, 2002; the gallery "gives the Native peoples of Indiana an ongoing presence in the Eiteljorg Museum. Art and images of historic and contemporary indigenous peoples, artifacts and interactive maps will communicate the breadth of Native cultures. The gallery will tell the story of the central Algonquian peoples with concentration on the Miami, the Potawatomi and the Delaware Nations." See also, *Mihtohseenionki (The People's Place) Teacher Resource Guide* (Indianapolis: Eiteljorg Museum of American Indians and Western Art, 2002).
43. Letter Sent, Dani Tippmann to John Vanausdall, June 14, 2002; John Vanausdall to Dani Tippmann, June 20, 2002; John Vanausdall to Dani Tippmann.
44. See, for example, *Generations: The Helen Cox Kersting Collection of Southwestern Cultural Arts*, edited by James H. Nottage (Indianapolis: Eiteljorg Museum of American Indians and Western Art, 2010).
45. The initial catalogue in the fellowship series was *Contemporary Masters, The Eiteljorg Fellowship for Native American Fine Art* (Indianapolis: Eiteljorg Museum of American Indians and Western Art, 1999). Seven volumes have followed. The latest includes a summary of the program's accomplishments. See, *Red: Eiteljorg Contemporary Art Fellowship, 2013*, edited by Jennifer Complo McNutt and Ashley Holland (Indianapolis: Eiteljorg Museum of American Indians and Western Art, 2013).

CHAPTER 8

Review and Final Thoughts

INTERPRETING NATIVE HISTORY AND CULTURE ***at Museums and Historic Sites*** summarizes some of the history between Native people, the United States, and museums. It outlines areas in which museum staff and trustees can work to improve policies and practices to build stronger relationships with Native communities. Contributors offered suggestions and practical advice from the field to enable museums to build or rebuild strong partnerships with Native communities based on respect, equality, and trust. Most importantly, ***Interpreting Native History and Culture at Museums and Historic Sites*** is about responsibility. The responsibility to understand and own any past mistakes and the responsibility to look to the future, to let go of fear, and envision shared partnerships with Native people that go beyond specific projects.

A Recap

Interpretation is a broad term with lots of meanings to different people, but in the museum profession, and for the purpose of this book, it is focused on the visitor and authority sharing. Interpretation for visitors needs to be meaningful: they need to be able to connect with the information being presented and understand it in reference to their own lives, values, and experiences. Interpretation also needs to be accurate and responsible, especially for the communities being represented in the interpretation.

Authority sharing is a concept that was revisited many times throughout the book and is vital for everyone within a museum to embrace if successful partnerships are to be made with Native people. Authority sharing honors that there are multiple ways of knowing about the past, about a culture, or about an issue. Each perspective and each person engaged in the process brings a unique experience to the table, and the group and the project can grow in unforeseen ways as a result. At times, it is appropriate to preference Native voice above other sources of knowledge because there exists an unbalanced relationship or understanding of the past that needs to be corrected. Non-Native academics and experts on history and Native culture can be accustomed to being recognized as an authority on certain subjects, such as archaeology, material culture, or history. It may be a new experience for them to be asked to share that authority with others, who often have a different or opposing view of the same topics. If necessary, listening sessions or research meetings may need to be conducted separately to ensure that all perspectives are shared and heard equally. For interpretation that represents best practices in this area, authority sharing is a key element to fully represent an issue, object, or event.

Partnerships Revisited

Authority sharing cannot take place if all involved do not trust one another and trust the process and outcome. To build trust, museum staff must take several steps, both internally, and with the communities with whom they seek to create partnerships. Staff activities to recognize and take responsibility for past mistakes are an important first step. Internal audits of past projects that involved Native people are a good way to start. Determine the successes and failures of past relationships and exhibit interpretation, focusing on the level to which the community was involved and if the relationships developed were maintained after the project was completed. Take a critical look at the collecting history of the museum, how the collections were acquired, and by whom. What types of objects are represented in the collection and what impact has this had on the communities from which these objects originate? Has there been any effort made to reconnect the objects with the community, to engage artists and historians, or to learn more about the objects from the creators? Recognize that understanding and taking responsibility for the history of the museum and its relations with Native people will never end; this will be an ongoing process as more information comes to light, as new relationships are developed, and to train incoming staff and board members.

Once internal audits are in process, the next step is to research the Native communities represented by the museum and come to understand who they are today, and more details about their history. Learn about their legal status and name, any history of removal and other traumatic experiences related to assimilation and genocide. Research the current issues faced by the tribe and how the government and elected officials are handling those issues. What topics are of pressing concern to the community? Recognize that the needs, timeline, and project of the museum will often be secondary to these issues.

Most importantly, museum staff and board need to realize that each tribe is different. Each tribe has a different set of values, experiences, hopes for the future, and cultural protocols and parameters with which they will prefer to engage with outsiders. Take the time to learn these, understanding that you are working with a sovereign nation that has been in continued existence for thousands of years. Address any cynicism or arguments to the contrary that might come up from museum representatives, including stereotypes about Native people and their retained status as sovereigns. Budget time and money to travel to Native communities to learn, to listen, and to buy products for the shop and collections.

Taking the Museum from Process to Operations

The goal in all of this is to move away from a series of steps and procedures that need to be followed to have strong partnerships with Native people and toward lasting organizational transformation that recognizes the authority of Native people to speak for themselves. This process is an opportunity for museums to transform themselves into safe spaces in which interpretation can become meaningful and transformative for visitors. That transformation can lead to better understanding of Native people, issues, and communities, which in turn can lead to a more equitable society in which Native people are not expected to assimilate into mainstream society and no longer have to fight to remain sovereign and are not criticized for doing so.

Museums are not limited by state educational standards and textbooks. We have the ability to interpret topics that are not discussed elsewhere, and because we have that ability, I would argue that it becomes a responsibility. Sharing authority between multiple perspectives and sources of knowledge creates critical thinkers. People who think critically about what they encounter have the skills to analyze new information and weigh the facts to determine accuracy. Museum visitors have responded favorably to changes in voice and authority sharing in museums, reinforcing the notion that visitors are prepared to learn new information and confront stereotypes in our museums.

The notion of decolonizing museums and museum interpretation takes us one step further in our understanding of best practices. "In my years studying exhibits that have been related to Native Americans, I have found that most contemporary museums are successful in producing exhibits that challenge the vanishing-Indian stereotype by emphasizing contemporary survival and sustained presence; but they have had limited success in presenting a hard-hitting analysis of colonization."[1] Embarking on a process of decolonization may be the next step for organizations that have strong partnerships with Native communities but want to go further.

There are aspects to this work that will impact the budget and time allocation of museum staff. Small museum staff and boards are often concerned with increases to budget or responsibilities. Taking the long view, this is a process—one that begins with internal work that does not cost money. Any effort to improve interpretation and practices will take an investment of staff and board time, but this planning and internal work often pays off with better visitor experience and stronger partnerships, which help balance some of the workload. Eventually, when a museum reaches the point of working with Native communities, budget adjustments will need to be made. This should not be a surprise; there is opportunity to raise additional funds to underwrite the work done with partners, including travel to and from reservations and purchasing works of art and craft from the community.

Because this is an ongoing process, and each relationship and each tribal community is different, museum staff need to keep up to date about changes in the field and in the communities they partner with. But forming partnerships based on honestly, transparency, and a commitment to equality will always be best practices.

Note

1. Amy Lonetree, "Museums as Sites of Decolonization Truth Telling in National and Tribal Museums" in *Contesting Knowledge Museums and Indigenous Perspectives*, edited by Susan Sleeper-Smith (Lincoln: University of Nebraska Press, 2009), 326.

APPENDIX 1

Timeline of Selected Federal Indian Policies, Laws, and Court Cases

THE FOLLOWING list of policies, laws, and court cases is a sampling of the vast and complex web of federal Indian law. There are many comprehensive resources available for more in-depth research. This list includes cases that are relevant to the museum profession and that are important to understand when building a relationship with Native people. Certainly, there will be laws, cases, and regional agreements that have not been included in this list. This exclusion in no way diminishes their importance, but rather reflects the limited nature of such timelines, and the incredible complexity of federal–Indian relations. I would encourage each reader to conduct research into his or her regional history to build on the foundation created here.

The timeline begins with the formation of the U.S. government. Obviously, American Indian relations with Europeans began hundreds of years before the formation of the United States. There are two reasons that this timeline begins with the United States. First, several European countries began sending explorers to the coastal regions of North America at slightly different times; imagine an ink stain seeping into the continent from all sides, at ragged, slightly varied intervals. Each country had a different philosophy for addressing Indian peoples' rights to land, religion, freedom, and life. Explorers from each country encountered different tribes, and as a result, there are differences in the ways in which the groups interacted. Summarizing this in any clear or comprehensive way is difficult and the subject of many other publications. Secondly, although there is no doubt that the United States inherited some policies that govern relations with Indian nations from the European powers that ceded territory, what impacts us today is federal Indian law.

When working with timelines, there are several resources on which I rely heavily. The first, ***American Indian Tribal Governments*** by Sharon O'Brien has a timeline of what she calls "Important Events in Indian History."[1] O'Brien begins her timeline before European contact, citing the League of the Iroquois and the All Indian Pueblo Council alliances, and then skips to 1492 and Columbus's landing, citing many significant events in addition to laws, treaties, and court cases. I supplement this timeline with more detailed information from *Documents of United States Indian Policy* edited by Francis Paul Prucha, and *American Indian Law in a Nut Shell* by William C. Canby, Jr.

Timeline

- 1777 United States forms and officially assumes control over Indian affairs.
- 1778 First treaty signed between the United States and Delaware Nation, establishing the system of nation-to-nation negotiations and acknowledging Indian sovereignty.
- 1787 The United States constitution is adopted, granting Congress the power to "regulate Commerce with foreign Nations, and among the several States, and with the Indian tribes."[2]
- 1789 The War Department assumes control over Indian affairs.
- 1790 The first Trade and Intercourse Act is passed, regulating trade with Indian nations under the authority of the U.S. government, not individuals or states. Established a system of trading posts where only traders licensed by the government could operate.
- 1803 Louisiana Purchase, the United States absorbs vast territory which is home to hundreds of Indian nations.
- 1815 United States starts negotiations with Indian tribes located north of the Ohio River and starts removing them to lands further west, thus beginning the practice of removing tribes from their territories. These negotiations lasted through 1825.
- 1823 *Johnson v. M'Intosh* Supreme Court case, first of three ruled by Chief Justice John Marshall, which combined, established the current status of Indian sovereignty in the United States. In this case, Marshall ruled that Indians could not own land but were merely occupants of the land. As tenants, they could transfer the right of occupancy to the occupying power only, not to states or individuals. Marshall cited the Doctrine of Discovery, a series of fifteenth-century Papal bulls that granted European explorers the power to claim title over lands not inhabited by Christian people.
- 1824 Bureau of Indian Affairs is established within the War Department.
- 1830 President Andrew Jackson signs the Indian Removal Act. By the end of his presidency, Jackson had signed into law almost seventy removal treaties, the result of which was to move nearly fifty thousand eastern Indians to Indian Territory in Oklahoma.
- 1831 *Cherokee Nation v. Georgia*, the second Supreme Court case decided by Chief Justice Marshall to establish the status of sovereignty for Native nations. Georgia began enacting laws that limited Cherokee sovereignty, so the tribe asked for an injunction, citing that Georgia's laws "go directly to annihilate the Cherokees as a political society."[3] The Cherokee argued that the Constitution recognized the tribe

as a sovereign foreign nation, and therefore not subject to Georgia's laws. Marshall ruled that tribes are not foreign nations but are "domestic dependent nations" functioning within the authority of the United States. Marshall left the door open for a follow-up suit to further define the rights of tribes.

- 1832 *Worcester v. Georgia*, the final case in the Marshall trilogy, in which Marshall clarifies that although tribes are domestic dependent nations, they do maintain a degree of sovereignty. Tribes have a protectorate relationship with the United States, and protection does not imply destruction of the protected. Essentially, this case preserved a degree of sovereignty for the tribes, acknowledging that they are more sovereign than states, but less sovereign than the federal government.
- 1848 Treaty of Guadalupe Hidalgo signed between the United States and Mexico ceding territory in California, New Mexico, Arizona, and several other western states. The United States agreed to grant citizenship to tribes living within this territory and never to remove them from their homelands.
- 1849 Bureau of Indian Affairs is transferred from the War Department to the Department of the Interior, marking a significant political shift in how Indian issues were managed. The United States had established its boundary from the east to the west coast, folding tribal lands into the territory. Indian nations were no longer outside of the political boundary of the United States, and therefore Indian relations were seen as internal affairs.
- 1868 last treaty signed with an Indian Nation. From this point on, Indian policy was made by acts of Congress and court cases, not treaties.
- 1879 Captain Richard Henry Pratt establishes Carlisle Industrial School, the first off-reservation boarding school with the intent of removing Indian children from the influences of their families and assimilating them into American society. The U.S. government operated more than one hundred boarding schools, and somewhere between twenty and thirty thousand Native American children went through the system, which was often administered and staffed by Christian religious organizations. The schools were notorious for their brutality and strict discipline.
- 1885 Major Crimes Act took jurisdiction away from the tribes for seven "major" crimes and placed it in the hands of the U.S. government. The list of crimes has since been expanded several times and now consists of fifteen offenses. The Major Crimes Act has removed the inherent right of Native people to apply their own laws and systems of justice on their own lands.
- 1888 Dawes Severalty Act, or the Allotment Act, divided up several reservations into individual allotments and assigned them to tribal members. The largest plots of land were granted to full-blooded Indians, and smaller plots were given to individuals with half- and quarter-percentage bloodlines. Many Native people, including most full-blood Indians, were deemed incompetent to manage their allotment, which was then turned over to an Indian agent. These agents often sold or leased the land without consent of the owner. The surplus land was removed from trust status and opened for settlement, often in land rushes. The act was aimed at destroying

communal ownership of land and making Indian people into farmers. Native people who received an allotment were also made citizens of the United States.

- 1906 Burke Act amended the Allotment Act to provide a twenty-five-year trust period on allotment lands. Unscrupulous land deals were common, and many Indian agents illegally sold or leased allotted lands. The trust period was to prevent transfer of ownership away from Native people.
- 1924 Indian Citizenship Act made all Native people citizens of the United States, ending a confusing period in which some Native people had citizenship and others did not.
- 1928 Meriam Report on "The Problem of Indian Administration" is released, calling attention to widespread poverty on Indian lands and calling for an end to the Allotment Act.
- 1934 Indian Reorganization Act ended allotment and created a means for tribes to regain a degree of independence and political sovereignty.
- 1935 Indian Arts and Crafts Board is established by Congress.
- 1946 Indian Claims Commission established with the purpose of ending claims to stolen Indian lands by making monetary compensation to the tribes.
- 1952 Indian Relocation Program started, creating funds to remove Indians from reservations and resettle them into cities.
- 1953 Termination Act systematically terminated the trust status for tribes that were economically self-sufficient.
- 1953 Public Law 280 granted limited criminal and civil jurisdiction over Indian tribes in California, Nebraska, Minnesota, Oregon, and Wisconsin.
- 1968 American Indian Civil Rights Act extended civil rights and liberties guaranteed by the Constitution to all reservation residents.
- 1971 Alaska Native Claims Settlement Act extinguished title to most of the state in exchange for forty-four million acres and a large cash settlement.
- 1972 Indian Education Act improved the quality of education on Indian reservations. The program was managed through a newly created Office of Indian Education.
- 1975 Indian Self-Determination and Education Assistance Act expanded tribal control over reservation programs. The act enabled tribal governments to manage their own housing, law enforcement, education, health care, social services, and community development programs reflective of tribal values and priorities.
- 1978 American Indian Religious Freedom Act passed to "protect and preserve for American Indians their inherent right of freedom to believe, express, and exercise their traditional religions."[4]
- 1978 Indian Child Welfare Act stopped the practice of adopting Native children out of Indian families and placing them with white families. Indian governments received a stronger voice in the process of adoption, advocating to place children in need with tribal or extended families, which reflected cultural values more closely.
- 1988 Indian Gaming Regulatory Act made it legal to operate gaming operations on trust lands in states where some form of gaming already exists. Tribes must apply

through a federal gaming commission to open a casino, making tribal gaming the most regulated in the world.

- 1990 Native American Graves Protection and Repatriation Act mandated that museums receiving federal funding are required to notify Indian tribes of human remains, funerary artifacts, and objects in collections pertaining to religions practices and cultural patrimony.
- 2000 Consultation and Coordination With Tribal Governments order signed, "in order to establish regular and meaningful consultation and collaboration with tribal officials in the development of Federal policies that have tribal implications, to strengthen the United States government-to-government relationship with Indian tribes, and to reduce the imposition of unfunded mandates upon Indian tribes."[5]
- 2009 Amendment of the Indian Arts and Crafts Bill passed as a truth-in-advertising law to limit the number of products being sold as "authentic Native" craft.
- 2010 Tribal Law and Order Act strengthened tribal courts, increased protection, and prevention of crime on Indian lands by improving training and communication for tribal and local law enforcement officers, as well as increased resources to protect Native women, who are statistically more likely to suffer physical and sexual abuse than other women.

Notes

1. Sharon O'Brien, *American Indian Tribal Governments* (Norman: University of Oklahoma Press, 1989), 299.
2. O'Brien, *American Indian Tribal Governments*, 301.
3. O'Brien, *American Indian Tribal Governments*, 57.
4. O'Brien, *American Indian Tribal Governments*, 310.
5. Excerpt from signing statement by Bill Clinton, for full statement and law see http://www.gpo.gov/fdsys/pkg/WCPD-2000-11-13/pdf/WCPD-2000-11-13-Pg2806-2.pdf.

Activity to Understand Stereotype and Bias

THERE ARE many activities similar to this that can help people recognize and understand personal bias and stereotypes prevalent in our society. The version here is inspired by something that was developed at the Abbe Museum in partnership with the Penobscot Cultural and Historic Preservation Department. The activity is designed to be conducted as a group and can be revisited many times as understandings about Native people change.

To get started you will need a quiet space for a group to gather, someone to take notes, someone to act as a facilitator, an easel with a note pad and pen, or a white board, and a few resource books, including *Do All Indians Live in Tipis: Questions and Answers from the National Museum of the American Indian*.

Introduction

Share the following information with the group before you start. This activity is meant to identify and understand the source of stereotypes about Native Americans in our society. Specific examples of how Native people are presented by outsiders in film, books, news, and other media changes quickly, but the underlying stereotypes often remain the same. This activity is designed to be flexible to these changes and isolate the various stereotypes and misunderstandings that exist among the staff, board, and visitors about Indian people, culture, and rights.

The discussion must be a safe space for people to ask questions and seek support from their peers. Each person will be asked to share terms or phrases that come to mind about Native people, but the group must recognize that this does not mean that the person necessarily believes in the words being shared. We have all been exposed to language, ideas, and images of Native people that we retain, whether or not we believe those things. The activity is not to spotlight a specific person and his or her opinions, but rather to create a list that represents a sampling of the kinds of things our society thinks and says about Native people.

The Activity

Begin by asking everyone in the group to picture a Native person or community in their head. Ask people to share words or phrases that come to mind when they hear the words ***Indian***, ***Native American***, or ***American Indian***. Write each term and phrase that is shared on the board for everyone to see. There are no wrong or right answers. Ideally, the list will be quite long. The facilitator may have to prompt people from time to time by asking questions, such as "What do Indians live in?" "What do they look like?" Although it may seem like these questions are leading, from my experience, people already have "tipis" and "long hair, braids, buckskin" in their minds; the questions are just pulling that information into the conversation. At first most of the terms will be neutral (e.g., ***feathers***, ***baskets***, ***tipis***, ***buffalo***, etc.), but as people become more comfortable, words like ***squaw***, ***savage***, and ***drunk*** may start to come out. This is good! Make sure these words are not censored because they are just as prevalent in our society as the neutral words, but less likely to be shared. The facilitator should try and pull out any popular culture references as well. When I hosted this activity while the ***Twilight*** series was popular, people often included shape shifting on the list.

This activity tends to wind down on its own because people run out of new terms or feel that the point has been made. Ask for any last words the group feels would be important to add to the list and then stop this part of the activity. For the next part, as a group, break the words down into three categories: positive, negative, and neutral. Each category represents stereotypes about Native people, negative being the most commonly understood. Positive and neutral stereotypes are just as damaging because they continue to set Native people apart, making them "other." Neutral stereotypes have a tendency to place Native people in the past because they are often focused on material culture and historic lifeways. This can be seen as an extension of colonialism, which is the continuing dominance and ownership over another people and their culture. It is true that everyone suffers from certain stereotypes, but for Native people the acceptance of these stereotypes, and the expectation that they should "get over it" is pervasive.

As the last part of the activity, define the terms using the resources available (including online). Discuss as a group where the stereotype came from, why it has remained, and how people have seen it represented in media, or more importantly, in your own museum. Create a list of take-away messages and practices to share with other staff, visitors, and stakeholders, and refer to them as you develop new interpretive materials related to Native Americans.

Index

Abbe:
museum, xiv, 39-40, 54, 61, 65-74, 125;
Robert, Dr., 65, 85
advisory committees, 45-48, 49, 51, 72, 73, 97, 107, 110
allotment, xii, 13n14, 26, 121-122
Allotment Act. *See* Dawes Severalty Act
American Alliance of Museums, 102
American Indian, defined, ix
anthropology (anthropologist), 51, 52, 58, 74
archaeology. *See* collections
assimilation, x, 7-8, 16, 31, 58, 116
Association of Tribal Archives, Libraries, and Museums, 62
appropriation, cultural and religious, 12, 19, 84, 88
authority sharing, xii, 20-21, 35-42, 82, 85, 98, 101, 115-116, 117

boarding schools, x, xii, 8, 10, 38, 121

Citizen Potawatomi Nation Cultural Heritage Center, xiii, 25-33
citizenship, 2, 13n14; Citizenship Act, 9, 122; through treaty, 6, 121
Cherokee Nation, 4, 5, 91, 106, 107, 120-121; *Nation v. Georgia*, 5, 120
collections, xi, xii, 15, 16, 19, 81-82, 83-84; archaeological, 58, 65-67; care, 28, 57, 59; collaborative, 61-62; ethnographic, 67; exhibiting, 37, 40-41, 43, 107-108; history of, 57-60, 116; management, 57, 67; planning, 67; online, 93; traditional conservation of, 30, 64
colonization, ix, x, 65, 72-74, 84, 102-103, 117
consultation, 10, 25, 27, 28, 30-31, 35, 38, 39, 43, 53, 86, 92, 105
Consultation and Coordination with Tribal Governments Order, 11, 123
contact zones, 94
cultural centers, vii, xii, 11, 17, 19, 28, 31-32, 35, 40, 41, 61, 64, 100
culture keeper, xii, 17

Dawes Severalty Act, 8, 121
decolonization:
defined, xiii; in museums, 42, 65, 68, 72-74, 98, 102-103, 117
Doctrine of Discovery, 2, 4, 120

education, x, xii, 1, 7, 8, 10-11, 17, 19 22, 25, 45, 47, 51, 62, 74, 77-85, 86, 87, 88, 89, 90, 91, 93, 97, 99, 101, 103, 104, 117
Eiteljorg Museum of American Indians and Western Art, 104-112
exhibits:
authority sharing, 20; collaborations, vii, xiii-xiv, 11, 16, 19-20, 27, 28, 29, 30, 31-32, 36, 38, 39-41, 43, 46, 47, 48, 49, 50, 54, 60, 61, 65, 69, 71, 72, 73-74, 82, 85, 87, 88, 92, 93, 97, 99, 104, 109; development, vii, xii

factions, 17, 37-38
federal Indian law, ix, 4, 6, 119
federal recognition, x,-xi, 13n16, 16-17, 29,
first person voice, xviii, 43, 50, 51-52, 53, 69, 74, 92-93, 100, 101

gap analysis, 60
gifting, 29

hands-on activities, 81, 84-85
human remains, xi, 11, 22, 63, 68, 70, 123

Indian, defined, ix
Indian Arts and Crafts Act, 11, 123
Indian Child Welfare Act, 10, 122
Indian Gaming Regulatory Act, 11, 122
Indian Reorganization Act, 9, 13n16, 122
interpretation, 18, 19; by anthropologists, xii; and authority sharing, xiii, 20, 35, 77, 79, 82, 85, 89, 93, 94, 98, 101, 103, 112, 115; in cultural centers, xii; defined, vii, 77, 99; of objects, 47; planning, 60, 68; and visitors, 99, 115
iPad, 91-92

Jackson, Andrew, 5-6, 120
Jefferson, Thomas, xi, 58
Johnson v. M'Intosh, 2, 4, 120

Major Crimes Act, 8, 121
Marshall, John, Chief Justice, 2, 4-6, 120-121
Monovocal, 88
museum shop, xi, 11, 69, 98, 99, 116,

National Museum of the American Indian, xiii, 18, 41, 48, 49, 50, 99, 101, 102, 105, 107, 109
Native American, defined, viii, ix-x
Native American Graves Protection and Repatriation Act (NAGPRA), vii, 11, 45, 57, 60, 61, 66, 70, 71, 73, 106
Natural History Museum of Utah, 43-54, 100, 101

Papal bulls. *See* Doctrine of Discovery
Polyvocal, 88-89
Portland Art Museum, 86-94
Potawatomi, 100-101, 105, 106, 108, 109, 110
Pratt, Richard Henry, 7, 121
Public Law 280, 10, 13n17, 122
Public Programming, 77-80

Religious Freedom Act, 10, 122
removal, 3, 6, 15-16, 26; Indian Removal Act, 5, 6, 120; working with removed tribes, 32, 116
Royal Proclamation, 3

school programs, 81-84, 85
self-determination, ix, 3, 10, 22; Self-Determination Act, 10, 122
Source Community, 62, 64
sovereignty, x, 97, 99, 103, 120; defined, 2; defined by the Supreme Court, 4-5, 120-121; in exhibits, 40, 80; limitations to, 6, 8; recognition, 16; restoration of, 11, 121, 122; termination of, 9-10; of tribal governments, 9
state-recognized tribes, x, 16
stereotypes, xi, xiii, xiv, 2, 12, 18, 36, 40, 41, 48, 64, 78, 80, 81, 83, 84, 85, 93, 99, 102, 116, 117, 125-126

termination, 3, 9; Termination Act, 9-10, 16, 122
Tilden, Freeman, viii, 81
tourist art, 59, 68, 69
Trade and Intercourse Act, 3, 8, 120
traditional conservation, 30
treaties, x, 6, 16, 120-121; defined, 2-3
Treaty of Guadalupe Hidalgo, 6-7, 121
Tribal Law and Order Act, 11, 123
tribal museums. *See* cultural centers

unrecognized tribes, 16, 25

vanishing race, xii, 1, 18, 44, 57, 58, 65, 78, 117

Wabanaki, ix, xvii, 39, 40, 65, 67-73
Worcester v. Georgia, 5, 121

youth, 7, 10, 17, 28, 53, 80, 86, 89, 91, 93

Zuni Cultural Center, 61

About the Author

Raney Bench has a B.A. in Native American Studies and a M.A. in Museum Studies. She has worked with Native communities and small museums throughout the United States for almost twenty years.